When You See A Sacred Cow... Milk It for All It's Worth

By Swami Beyondananda
with Steve Bhaerman

Aslan Publishing
P.O. Box 108
Lower Lake, CA 95457

Published by
Aslan Publishing
P.O. Box 108
Lower Lake, CA 95457
(707) 995-1861

For a free catalog of all our titles, or to order more
copies of this book please call (800) 275-2606

Library of Congress Cataloging-in-Publication Data

Beyondananda, Swami.
    When you see a sacred cow—milk it for all it's worth / by Swami
Beyondananda with Steve Bhaerman.
        p. cm.
    ISBN 0-944031-48-X : $9.95
    I. Bhaerman, Steve.   II. Title.
PN6162.B549   1993
818'.5407—dc20

                                                                93-6317
                                                                CIP

Sections in this book have been quoted from Swami Beyondananda's
Driving Your Own Karma: Swami Beyondananda's Tour Guide to Enlightenment,
published by Destiny Books, an imprint of Inner Traditions International, Ltd.,
One Park Street, Rochester, VT 05767.

On page 9: "WHO PUT THE BOMP (In The Bomp Bomp Bomp)" by Barry Mann and
Gerry Goffin (c) 1961 Renewed 1989 SCREEN GEMS-EMI MUSIC INC.
All Rights Reserved. International Copyright Secured. Used by permission.

Cover illustration by Peter Sinclair
Printed in USA
10 9 8 7 6 5 4 3 2 1

Table of Contents

~~~~~Introduction~~~~~

On Milking the Sacred Cow

Ever since I can remember, I've been asking questions. At first they were very simple questions, questions like "Could you change my diaper?" and "Can I try that other breast for a while?" But as my natural curiosity about the world awakened, I began to ask deeper questions: When did time begin? When will it end? Do you turn the clock backward or forward for daylight savings time? Do we have any time-outs left, or will the clock just keep running? And of course I pondered the meaning of Life. Did life have any true significance, or were we simply the Comedy Channel for the Gods?

And so I began my search for someone wiser than myself. Which was pretty easy in those days, for I was a young Oklahoma farm boy still wet behind the ears (this was before guys used hair dryers). I knew enough to know I didn't know much but not enough to know how much I didn't know. I developed a ravenous appetite for knowledge, and had eaten nearly half the philosophy books in the local library when my first mentor, the great Native American shaman Broken Wind, took me aside to tell me I was going about it the wrong way. "Your hunger for knowledge is admirable, young one, but it must be preceded by the thirst for wisdom."

I found this advice tremendously helpful. Thereafter I would shred the texts and combine them with water in a blender. Needless to say, I found the information infinitely more digestible that way. I devoured text after text until I had expanded my mind so much I could no longer fit through my door. My folks thought they would have to call in a shrink, but fortunately Broken Wind once again came to the rescue. He taught me gastral projection, a technique I still find helpful for crowd-dispersion.

I began to think that maybe I had been taking the wrong approach to enlightenment. Perhaps I had gotten too left-brained about the whole thing. Maybe it was time I developed my intuitive self. I even considered enrolling in a class on "Drawing On the Right Side of Your Brain," but at the last minute I copped out. I just couldn't bring myself to shave half my head.

I was on the verge of giving up seeking entirely and just getting a regular job at the local karma wash when I heard about a spiritual master who used rock 'n' roll to teach life's great truths. Perhaps you've heard of him—Baba Oom Mow Mow. I already had read about the power music had to change consciousness. It seems that back in 1959, scientists at Johns Hopkins University divided young tomato plants into two groups. For twelve hours a day, they played Mozart to the first group of plants. The other group heard Elvis for the same amount of time. The results were truly amazing. After six weeks, the Mozart group had grown straight and tall. The Elvis group had grown sideburns.

But anyway, in Baba Oom Mow Mow I found an individual whose spiritual journey could inspire my own. Born Zach Lee Wright in Knoxville, Tennessee, he was the son of the noted preacher Saul Wright. Although young Zach's first love was rock 'n' roll, this kind of music was forbidden in the family, and the youngster was encouraged to study only traditional, church and classical music. This he did half-heartedly and without distinction. Records show he attended Misty Point Junior College, where he majored in band conducting and flunked out.

After leaving home, he drifted from one rock band to another leading the honky-tonk life. Fortunately, fate stepped in (and when fate steps in something, it never fails to track it right across your karma). One night, Zach was playing at a bar in Louisville as lead guitarist for the heavy metal band Meaty Ochre (not to be confused with the even more obscure Cajun Zydeco band "Meaty Okra") and he accidentally slobbered some beer onto his amplifier cord. The resulting shock blew all of his circuits, and for once his lack of ability saved his life. Had he been a better conductor, he would have died for sure.

Life was never the same after that. As Zach would say later, "Some folks have been touched by the hand of God. Me, He knocked upside the head." Then and there he gave up the smoky bar scene and foreswore hard drink (easy drink he still partakes of, however). He moved to a simple cabin made of earth and wood (his friend Johnny B. Goode had recently left it to go to the city) and began to formulate what he calls the Golden Rule of Rock 'N' Roll, which can be summed up as "Do wop unto others as you would have them do wop unto you." Taking the name "Baba Oom Mow Mow," he is known for composing and performing popular tunes that leave no chakra unturned. His best known hits include: "Love Is Like An I Ching In My Heart," "Everybody Needs Samadhi Sometime," "B'hai B'hai Love," "Swami Said There'll Be Days Like This," "Zen He Kissed Me," "Yanni Get Angry," "You Ascend Me," and "Hang On Sufi."

By the time I met Baba Oom Mow Mow, he was living in semi-retirement devoting most of his time to putting the Akashic records on CD. The rest of the time he and several other old guys were playing in a '50s revival band called Ancient Grease. When I told him I was seeking the answers to Life's Great Mystery, he scratched his pompadour and said, "You know, once at a Fabian Society meeting Georgie Shaw told me if you repeat a question enough the answer will come." He excused himself and went into his archives of 45s. He came out with a copy of "Who Put the Bomp In The Bomp-Ba-Bomp-Ba Bomp?" and instructed me to listen to it until I discovered the Meaning of Life. Three weeks later after nearly 10,000 spins the record was worn out and so was I.

I stumbled into Baba Oom Mow Mow's sanctum and babbled the mantra that had worn a permanent groove in my consciousness: "Bomp-ba-bomp-ba-bomp, rama-lama-ding-dong, dip-da-dip-da-dip, boogety-boogety-shoo."

"That's it," said the Great Master. "You got it."

"That's it? 'Bomp-ba-bomp-ba-bomp, rama-lama-ding-dong, dip-da-dip-da-dip, boogety-boogety-shoo' is the meaning of life? It just doesn't make any sense."

"Exactly right," he nodded. "That's the brilliance of rock 'n' roll. In a society that hasn't made any sense for at least two generations, rock has given us the language to tell it like it is. I mean, imagine you're a kid back there in the '50s and you're in school and they're having a shelter drill where you put your head under your desk and that's supposed to save you from nuclear attack? Do you see where 'Sha-na-na-na, sha-na-na-na-na' or 'Ya-da-da-da-da-da-da-da-da-da sh-boom, sh-boom' might make more sense than anything your teacher might tell you?"

I couldn't argue with his logic, and yet there was something missing. "Well," I said, "if life's meaning can be summed up in a series of nonsense syllables, does life have any purpose? Is there any reason why we are here in the first place?"

"Well, that's a slightly different question," he said. Baba Oom Mow Mow once again went deep within his archives and emerged with a dusty LP. "Here you will find your answer," he said handing me a copy of *Liberace Plays Little Richard.*

I listened to this obscure album religiously for months. And then one night it came to me, just as the Prince of Glitter was putting a final glissando on "Tutti Frutti." The secret of life is astoundingly simple. *Every human being secretly wants to be a great piano player!* To test my hypothesis, I asked everyone I knew. Sure enough, each and every one would have given their last Haagen Dasz bar to be another Artur Rubinstein, Bruce Hornsby or even a Fats Domino. Excitedly, I rushed into Baba Oom Mow Mow's quarters to tell him of my discovery. I had to wait in silence until the "Hullaballoo" re-run he was watching was over, and then I spilled it. "Oh, Hollied One," I shouted. "I have found the secret of life, I've found the secret of life! See, every human being wants to be a great piano player!"

The grizzled rocker looked at me with quiet bemusement and said, "Calm down, calm down. Your discovery is nothing new. Sigmund Freud came up with the same thing back in 1905. He called it Pianist Envy."

This was a shock to me since I'd always heard Freud was hung up on sax. Guess I'd have to go back and listen to my Pink Freud* albums. At any rate, I sensed that my time with Baba Oom Mow Mow was coming to an end. This suspicion was confirmed when he played one final record for me, "Hit The Road, Jack."

"Well I guess if you say so," I said reluctantly, "I'll have to pack my things and go."

"That's right," he said. And he closed the door behind me.

So there I was, my children. I had exhausted all the great teachers I knew of, and they had exhausted me. Perhaps instead of going from teacher to teacher, I needed to find one guru and settle down. And it wasn't long after that that I found exactly what I was seeking. I was looking through one of those supermarket tabloids reading a fascinating article about how Elvis had secretly made a martial arts instruction video back in the early '70s which was about to be released to the public as "Chi Kung A La King", when I spotted the ad that would change the course of my life. "We're Looking For People Who Want To Draw . . . On Higher Consciousness", the headline said. And underneath was the address for Famous Gurus School in New York. The testimonial that finally clinched it for me read: "Loved your leadership training. Please send followers."

I eagerly wrote away for information, and that is how I first learned about Harry Cohen Baba, the Garment Center Saint. Oh, yes. It brings

---

* Obviously a Floydian slip—Ed.

a warm glow to my heart chakra to think of this great being. He was born into a family of tailors on the Lower East Side, and at a very early age demonstrated remarkable healing powers. Whenever an item of torn or frayed clothing was brought into his presence, he would wave his hand over the garment, say a few loving words like "Pull yourself together" or "Don't be 'frayed," and magically the garments would be healed.

Naturally, word of the youngster's remarkable gift spread throughout the Lower East Side and families would come in droves to have their old garments made like new. This created a conflict in young Harry Cohen's family. His religious grandfather equated this kind of jean-splicing with playing God. Not to mention the fact that Harry was putting everyone out of business. (This entire episode is explained in far greater detail in Harry Cohen Baba's autobiography, *Clothes Encounters With The Supernatural*.) Filled with compassion for his family yet unwilling to give up his God-given power, Harry Cohen left to seek his own way. There followed a period of some fifteen years where Harry Cohen renounced not only his powers and his family, but clothing in general. He became a follower of the prophet Nuddha, and was a practicing Nuddhist. For many years, he moved from camp to camp wearing nothing but a little skullcap to protect his bald spot from the sun's rays. Finally, one day he decided to take stock. "I'm nearly 40 years old, and what do I have to show for it? Granted, I got a terrific tan—and no unsightly bikini lines—but look at me. Nuddhism has left me totally unsuited for life. I've run away from my powers for too long. It's time to renounce being a renunciate!"

And so Harry Cohen became Harry Cohen Baba and began to teach the Garment Center Creed: "As a man sews, so shall he reap." He returned to the Lower East Side and his family, and he applied his magical powers in the family tailor shop where he toiled needlelessly. There he attained his greatest happiness, for in his own words, "Success in the world is nothing until you've patched things up with your own family."

I also discovered the Garment Centered One came from a long line of spiritual masters. This was not widely known because spiritual masters will never stand in a long line if they can help it. This spiritual lineage is known as Men of the Cloth, and needless to say they are a very close-knit group. Their specialty is using the spiritual to heal the material. As Harry Cohen Baba's own guru, Yeshivananda, used to say, "Life is a situation comedy that will never get cancelled, and the reason why we are put in the material world is to get more material."

And so each year Yeshivananda would make two pilgrimages to the mountains to obtain the finest material. In the summer, he would go to the Catskills for spiritual material. Levity, he believed, would make him lighter. And in the fall, he would go to the Himalayas for cloth, for he was the most renowned sari maker in all of New York City. Truly he had the gift of garb. It was said that his work was so much in demand that women had to take numbers and line up around the block for their traditional Indian dresses. Each time he would pick a number, he would look around the small shop and sing, "Whose sari now?" It is believed that this was the first wrap song.

And you know, the philosophy of these Men of the Cloth is truly applicable today when so many people are shedding their old habits and finding out what fits for them. In the beginning, they say, was the "Naked Truth"—and humankind has been dressing up the truth ever since. This fabrication is all right as long as we remember the words of the Garment Centered Ones: "Don't accept hand-me-down religion. Don't tailor your beliefs to someone else's fashion. Don't wait to be fitted into some uniform. Suit yourself!"

And so, having read all I could find about Harry Cohen Baba and his lineage, I decided to meet the Master himself. When I arrived in New York, I was told that the revered master could be found at his usual table at Louie's Finer Deli on the Lower East Side. I spotted his glowing aura from across the room, and I rushed to his table where he was devouring a pastrami sandwich and washing it down with Dr. Brown's Cel-Ray Tonic.

"Oh, Garment Centered One," I said reverently. "Please tell me. What is the meaning of life?"

"Digesting," he replied, his mouth full, barely looking up from his plate.

"That's it? Just sitting here and eating food is the meaning of life?" I asked, greatly disappointed.

"Who said anything about food?" he replied. "I said the meaning of life is *die jesting*. We all gotta die someday, so we may as well die jesting. And you truly never know when the old Grin Reaper may show up, so I suggest that you start jesting right away."

And so it was that Harry Cohen Baba initiated me into the ancient Chinese path of Fu Ling, and instructed me in that noble path's One Commandment: *When you see a sacred cow, milk it for all it's worth.*

I must admit at the beginning I was puzzled. "What do you mean by milking the sacred cow?" I asked.

"Look, boychick," he said, "it used to be these sacred cows we hear about brought nourishment. You've heard of the 'milk of human kindness?' You think that's just an expression? Where do you think it came from? In the ancient times, we just let spirit nourish us in its Motherly way, and we lived in Udder Bliss. But then someone got the bright idea that we needed words to describe the experience, and rules to live by. And somewhere back there—it must have been during the Age of Taurus—the sacred cow got overrun by the bull. They don't call those decrees Papal Bulls for nothing, you know."

"Now wait a minute," I interrupted. "Don't you think Christians might interpret that last statement as a Papal smear and take offense?"

"Why should they?" the Garment Centered One replied. "Jesus wasn't responsible for those decrees. Like most great Masters, He taught that each of us has to find our own whey. But you know how people are. Instead of doing the milking and extracting the cream himself, the average guy would rather be formula-fed. After generations of this pasteurized, homogenized, 2% spirituality, the body politic has lapsed into a deep cattlepsy. And without a connection to Spirit, it's been easy for a powerful few to bulldoze Mother Nature and seek immortality in their own creations. I think Freud called this the unresolved edifice complex. But fortunately," he said, poking me in the ribs with a kosher dill, "there are Comic-kazes."

"Comic-kazes?"

"Yes. It is the duty of the Comic-kaze to use humor as a gentle yet effective laughsitive to purge the bull, restore regularhilarity, and remind us that life is indeed a joke—where God laughs *with* us, not *at* us. Anyway, as a Comic-kaze initiated into the path of Fu Ling, you are being entrusted to teach the herd to develop a meaningful relationship with their Significant Udder. And in so doing, you will help turn addictions into benedictions, and pain into champagne."

And so it was that I became part of the FUNdamentalist Revival, the *real* old time religion where the Fun comes before the mental and celebration outweighs cerebration. We FUNdamentalists realize that Nonjudgment Day is at hand and the best way to illuminate darkness is to make light of it. And so, dear reader, may this book initiate you into this Pro-Laugh movement that will provide the levity to overcome all the gravity of the world. Go now, and milk each moment for every last drop of joy and insight. Revel without a cause. Live life to the foolest. And do it till the cows come home. May the Farce be with you.

Swami Beyondananda

1

I Never Metaphysical Question I Didn't Like

In my travels over the past several years, I have noticed there is a lot of confusion on the planet. According to a recent *USA Today* poll, 65% of Americans admit to feeling confused—and the rest aren't sure. And it's no wonder, what with all the talk of planetary upheaval and Earth changes and the like. One day we read about some mystic who is predicting chaos and destruction. The next day there is another mystic who is saying we are on the verge of a peaceful transformation that will bring heaven on Earth. Who do we believe, anyway?

The answer is simple—what you believe is up to you. See, there are two kinds of mystics in the world—the optimystics and the pessimystics. The pessimystics tend to be more realistic, but the optimystics are happier and live longer. I'll give you an example. The pessimystics have been predicting the poles are going to shift. The optimystics say the Poles have already shifted, and the Czechs, the Germans and even the Russians have followed suit. The good news is, we're all going to shift. Because this is not the 1980s anymore, this is the 1990s. And there is a new slogan for the '90s: SHIFT Happens!

So if you have this feeling that the shift has already hit the fan, relax—because you're not alone. If you started out seeking paradise and found paradox instead, welcome to the club. If you finally understand that all of the answers are already in you—only you forgot the question—take heart. Yes, if you're totally bewildered, the Swami has good news for you. Consider this book your bewilderness survival manual, guaranteed to answer all of your questions—including many you wouldn't dream of asking.

• • •

Dear Swami:

I have a problem. Flying is very uncomfortable for me because I am deathly afraid that someone might have a bomb on the plane. I realize the odds of this actually happening are slim, but I feel so powerless about the whole thing. Isn't there something I can do to have more control over the situation?

Dee Zaster,
Misty Point, North Carolina

Dear Dee:

Fortunately, I've made a thorough study of the situation you are referring to and I have good news. The odds of someone having a bomb on your plane are about one in 600,000—pretty remote. The odds of two people having a bomb on the same plane are really remote—about one in three billion. So my advice to you is simple. Next time you fly, take a bomb with you.

• • •

Dear Swami:

I've got to know. Oh great Swami, what's the next big thing?

Anita Fixx,
Redondo Beach, California

Dear Anita:

You know, I never make predictions. And there are two reasons for this. First, I don't want to lose my non-prophet status. And second, I remember what my beloved guru Harry Cohen Baba used to say: "Anything can be predicted, but nothing can be predicted accurately." Think about it. What about all those annual predictions you see every January in those trashy tabloids? Has any one of those ever come true? You see, there are simply too many variables. It is like trying to predict the weather. All of these expensive scientific instruments and one butterfly fart can have an unpredictable ripple effect. And predicting how life will turn out is the same way. Even the great Nostradamus, as deep as his wisdom and understanding was, still failed to predict the last three NBA champions.

So given that disclaimer, I will simply offer my opinion about the Next Big Thing. It will be multiple personalities. Yes, we are all multiple personalities. See, it all got started with the inner child work. Once you've discovered your inner child, that's when the work begins. You have to potty train your inner child, right? Then you start meeting these other inner beings. Your inner grandmother. Your inner uncle. Your inner cousins from Toledo. Pretty soon, you're having regular inner family reunions. Somebody has to feed all these people, so you start looking around for an inner somebody who has a marketable skill. That's where the multiple personality work comes in. All you got to do is find the inner millionaire, and you're set for life. And if that doesn't work, no problem. You can still claim all these other inner beings as dependents.

• • •

Dear Swami:

I guess I'm just a sucker for psychics because I just can't pass one by without getting a reading. What's worse is, I make important decisions based on those readings, which has led to some disastrous consequences. Case in point: Two years ago, a seer told me I would make a fortune if I invested all my money in disposable diapers. This I did, and at first my stocks went up steadily. But then a report was released saying disposable diapers are a threat to the environment because they take up to 500 years to decompose—and that they're actually more costly than diaper services. Next thing you know, a couple of states have outlawed them, and my stocks are virtually worthless. So I returned to the seer and she shrugged as if to say, "So sue me." My question is, can I? Is there such a thing as psychic malpractice? Should I bother? Or is there some other lesson to be learned from this?

> Ian Dulge,
> Aspen, Colorado

Dear Ian:

Even though there is much to be seen with the eyes closed, there are also times to keep your eyes open. Had you learned more about the nature of disposables, you might not have thrown so much of your disposable income down the disposal. Take responsibility for how you chose to dispose of your money. Forget the lawsuit. After all, this is the new age and seer-sucker suits are definitely out of style.

• • •

Dear Swami:

I read recently that you have mastered the esoteric art of Baseball Card Reading. Why baseball? Is there some kind of metaphysical significance to the game?

> Boog Alou,
> Miami, Florida

Dear Boog:

Oh, yes. Baseball—or Tai Cobb as it is known in spiritual circles—is a very metaphysical game. As in life, it is the object of the game to journey around the bases and return home. And like genuine enlightenment, it is a team effort. Although it is the home run hitter who gets the recognition, the Most Valuable Player is often the so-called Bunting Sattva who sacrifices his own opportunity to return home in order to "move the runners along." Like the Universe, baseball transcends time itself. For if there is perfect batting or perfect defense, the game can actually go on infinitely. A favorite koan or meditation of Tai Cobb practitioners involves a mythical game between the San Francisco Giants and the Los Angeles Dodgers where Darryl Strawberry is playing outfield for the Dodgers. The Giants come to bat first, and they are so perfect that they are never retired. This meditation, by the way, has been immortalized in the song, Strawberry Fields Forever.

• • •

Dear Swami:

For about a year, I've been hearing about the 11:11—supposedly an invisible doorway in consciousness that allows us to pass through to a higher dimension. Apparently, this doorway is only to be opened for a brief time. Now I find out that the 11:11 happened in January, and I missed it. Tell me, Swami is there any chance something like this will come around again in my lifetime?

Ewell Nevenow,
Mesa, Arizona

Dear Ewell:

You're in luck! This coming July, there will be another opportunity to stroll through the portals of enlightenment. It's called the 7:11, and unlike the 11:11 it's open all the time.

• • •

Dear Swami:

I keep hearing about all those UFO abductions. Are these stories true? And if so, is there anything we can do about it?

Ida Wanna,
Berwyn, Pennsylvania

Dear Ida:

I'm afraid those stories are true, and there really isn't much we can do about it. Sure, we could go back to having all aliens register with the government every January, but the paperwork would do us in long before they could. Yes, we are being experimented on, but it shouldn't be surprising to us. You see, just like us humans, many extraterrestrials believe in experimenting on less evolved life forms to improve the quality of their own lives. And that is why they are using us to test their cosmetics.

• • •

Dear Swami:

My softball team has won 14 games in a row, which is great. Except that I believe that we're winning in part because of my "lucky socks," and I've been afraid to take them off since our first win. This wouldn't be too bad, except that we only play one game a week. So I've been wearing the same socks every day for three months. Needless to say, this has created some problems. My girlfriend told me to call her after the playoffs are done, my boss has insisted that I can accomplish just as much work if I stay home, and the police have come by three times looking for the dead body. Even though I'm an otherwise rational guy, I truly believe that if I stopped wearing these socks, we'd lose. Can inanimate objects really bring good luck, or am I just a superstitious fool?

Jim Schooze,
Delaware, Ohio

Dear Jim:

This concept of "good luck" is indeed a metaphysical puzzle. And since I never metaphysical puzzle I didn't like, I will try to shed some light on it for you. Many years ago, while I was under the tutelage of Harry Cohen Baba, the Garment Center Saint, I walked into his inner sanctum and was surprised to find a horseshoe above the door. "Garment Centered One," I asked reverently, "can it be true that a man of your learning and wisdom actually believes that a horseshoe can bring good luck?"

"Of course not," he laughed. "I think the entire notion is utter nonsense."

"But if you don't believe in it," I asked, "why did you put it up there?"

"Because, boychick, it works whether you believe in it or not."

• • •

Dear Swami:

I have heard that some spiritual masters who live in the Himalayas are so spiritually evolved that they no longer need to eat food and can exist on breath alone. Is this true?

Hy Kalonik,
Ozone Park, New York

Dear Hy:

This is true. I was recently in the Himalayas and I went to a breatharian restaurant. Naturally, they serve no food there. But the atmosphere is terrific! While I was there, I was puzzled to see these beings walking around with clothespins on their noses. I later found out they were fasting.

• • •

Dear Swami:

I have lived a life of wanton debauchery, and my preacher tells me I'm doomed. Is there anything I can do to keep from burning in Hell?

Jacques Kitsch,
Vancouver, British Columbia

Dear Jacques:

Yes, there is. Number 40 sunscreen.

• • •

Dear Swami:

I've been wondering. Can you tell me what animals think about all day? Do they meditate?

Phil Ossifer,
Mt. Shasta, California

Dear Phil:

No, I can't tell you what animals think about. But I can give you some idea of what they don't think about:

1. Dogs almost never wake up in the morning and say, "God, I have terrible breath! Gimme a carton of Certs now, or I'll be too embarrassed to lick anyone today."

2. Cows don't think, "Now let's see. Where can I poop? No, can't poop there—the farmer might step in it. Can't poop here. I might step in it. Oh, what the heck. I'll just hold it in."

3. Dolphins don't think, "We should go out and capture some humans, keep them in air tanks and make them do stupid pet tricks like catching hamburgers in their mouths."

4. *Cats don't think, "I know I'm not supposed to be on the table, but I can't help it. I do it, and then I feel so guilty. I wonder if there are any support groups for something like this."*

Consequently, animals don't need to meditate.

• • •

Dear Swami:

I understand the process of enlightenment can be summed up in just three words. Is that so?

> Ray Zendetra,
> Sandusky, Ohio

Dear Ray:

Yes. Ego, egoing, egone.

• • •

Dear Swami:

I have a friend who just drives me nuts. No matter what disaster happens, global or personal, she insists that everything is "just perfect." How can I find out if she's really that enlightened or just in denial?

> Sonya Buttons-Zahn,
> Elgin, Illinois

Dear Sonya:

Next time she says everything is perfect, tell her, "That's great because I just stepped in some dog perfection outside and I hope you don't mind me tracking it on your rug." The expression on her face will answer your question.

• • •

Dear Swami:

I keep reading this stuff about the healing power of laughter, but I just don't see it. Life is fraught with tragedy, disappointment, frustration, pain. In all the focus on laughing our way through adversity, I see nothing but denial. War, disease, starvation? Frankly, I am not amused. If the great Swami can prove that God indeed does have a sense of humor, I'll eat my hardbound copy of *War and Peace*.

> Hugh Morliss,
> Meredith, New Hampshire

Dear Hugh:

Let me tell you a true story which should lay to rest any doubts about the Creator's sense of humor. As you may know, the Swami now lives Somewhere In Texas on a spread called the Cattlelack Ranch (so named because there isn't a cow on the place). Although we lack cattle, there is no scarcity of raccoons, whom I have found to be lifelong criminals without a smidgen of remorse. I must admit that when the last pack of raccoons decimated the garden, the thought crossed my mind that all the Swami's disciples would look terrific in Davy Crockett hats.

But being a humane kind of guy, I went to the Humane Society and picked up several live traps. The man there told me that I must capture the animals live, then drop them off in the woods about 15 miles away. This I did, and just as I was pulling into my driveway, I saw someone else—with similar humane intentions—dropping off a family of raccoons on my land. (Incidentally, Hugh, you have my permission to substitute the Reader's Digest condensed version of War and Peace *for the hardbound. Same nutritional content, half the calories. "Bon appetit.")*

• • •

Dear Swami:

Are there any absolutes in this world?

Jeanetta Fisch,
Springfield, Massachusetts

Dear Jeanetta:

Absolutely not. Everything is relative. It is like the billionaire who comes down to breakfast, and his wife asks him how he's feeling. "I feel like a million bucks," he says. And she says, "Oh, my goodness. What's wrong?"

• • •

Dear Swami:

I'm mad as hell and I'm not gonna take it anymore! Ever since I was a child, I've been told that if I was good and said my prayers and so on, that God's blessings would rain down on me. Sure, there would be some adversity but those would be blessings in disguise. Well let me tell you, my blessings have been so disguised that they're virtually unrecognizable. Not a day goes by that the bird of paradise doesn't drop a juicy one on my new suit. The traditional religions are bad enough, but this "new age" claptrap really takes the cake. Imagine this: Some lady told me the other day that I actually chose everything that happens in my life! Before I was born I made a contract with God and I agreed to have all these "lessons." Well I must have been the victim of false advertising, because I know I didn't ask for this. Swami, you know about these things. Is there any way I can get out of the contract?

Ike Witt,
Flushing, New York

Dear Ike:

It's obvious you got a lousy deal. If I were you, I'd get myself a good Universal lawyer and I'd sue. It's already being done by others, so why shouldn't you give it a shot? I've read several articles lately from all across the country where people who feel they've been misled or gotten a bum deal are suing God. Now of course, God himself carries very little cash—and you know how hard those Swiss banks are to get into. So people are doing the next best thing—suing religious organizations. I have an article right here about some guy who's suing the Catholic Church because he claims Hail Marys "simply don't work." In his deposition, he goes on to say that Hail Marys were not adequately tested before they were put out on the market, and calls the Church's miraculous claims "misleading."

So I can only encourage you to press your suit (but be sure to get the dry cleaners to remove the bird droppings first). I should warn you, however, that God uses only the best lawyers—part of an elaborate trade agreement with Satan—and the settlement could be delayed for years, centuries even. On the positive side, God has a reputation for being merciful—so there is always the chance he will hear your plaintiff cry and settle out of court.

• • •

Dear Swami:

What can you tell me about walk-ins? It's my understanding that people sometimes go through a serious crisis or illness, or even a near-death experience—and their life is transformed to the point where they even think they are being inhabited by a different soul. Is this true? Can you shed some light on this phenomenon?

Dawn Bacilli,
San Anselmo, California

Dear Dawn:

The human body was designed as a single-occupancy dwelling, but occasionally there are comings and goings without a formal change in the leasing agreement. Channeling, for example, is a temporary sublet, although sometimes these pesky entities move in all their furniture and you have to call in the Higher State Patrol to evict them. Sometimes the original soul says, "You know what? This is a lousy movie, I already know the ending, and I'm not gonna sit through it. I'm leaving." This is known as a "walk-out," and if there happens to be a disembodied soul standing outside the theater, he might say, "Hey, do you mind if I use your ticket?" And boom. You have a walk-in.

There'a another way that walk-ins can walk in. Perhaps you've seen these little ads for out-of-body travel clubs? I would be very cautious about these. First thing they do is get you intoxicated on spirit. One thing leads to another, and you wake up and find yourself in some stranger's body. So if you ever wake up with this kind of psychic hangover and say to yourself, "I'm just not myself today," you probably aren't.

• • •

Dear Swami:

I know you've probably been asked this before, but I've got to have an answer. What is the meaning of life?

Reed Undant,
Chicago, Illinois

Dear Reed:

It is true. Many people have asked me this, and they usually forget to specify whether they are talking about Life (the magazine) or Life (the cereal). Anyway, I will give you my up-to-the-minute answer, one I have gleaned from one of the most celebrated football coaches in all of Texas, Linus Grimmage: Life is like football. If you want to be Quarter-

29

back, you must first find your Center. Also, if you are displeased with your place in the standings this time around, do not despair. You get first-round draft choice your next lifetime. Remember that in life as in football, it is you who determines your position. You can be a tight end if you want, or you can be a wide receiver. It is up to you. Finally, in your quest to make great gains, be easy on yourself. Know that for every fumble, there will be a recovery.

• • •

Dear Swami:

Is it possible for us to fail God?

Bernie Turner Lee,
Roswell, Georgia

Dear Bernie:

You're way ahead of me. I didn't even know we were grading Him.

• • •

Dear Swami:

Are you a legitimate Swami? Also, do you consider yourself a fully-realized being?

Doc Trinaire,
Walnut Creek, California

Dear Doc:

Of course I'm a legitimate Swami! After all, both my parents were married—to each other, I might add. As for being fully-realized, I believe we are all realized, but we don't become fully realized until we fully realize it.

• • •

Dear Swami:

A lot of school systems nowadays are dealing with the issue of Evolution vs. Creationism. What's your theory on the origin of life?

Fulana Hill,
Philadelphia, Pennsylvania

Dear Fulana:

I find it admirable that so many scientists and religionists have been discussing the origin of the Universe and trying to reconcile both the scientific and the religious points of view. In fact, one popular theory currently making the rounds is that God created the Universe for His 7th grade science project—and got a C.

But to me, the most scientifically and metaphysically accurate creation theory comes from the great Native American teacher, Broken Wind. In the beginning, the story goes, there was Father Sky, who was alone for many, many eons. One day, He found Himself feeling very bored. Since there was no TV in those days, He decided to create the Universe as his very own Home Entertainment Center. The problem was, Father Sky was a real idea guy, but not much on handling details. He realized He needed a partner in this venture. He was too impatient to use the personals ads—the newspaper would not be invented for another 800 billion years—so He decided instead to use the Law of Attraction. He would simply think of the kind of partner He desired, and that Being would show up.

Sure enough, in a matter of seconds (we speak metaphorically here since time would not actually exist until later the next week), a Being materialized, and so breathtaking was this Being's beauty that Father Sky forgot all about His plans for a Home Entertainment Center. "Wh-wh-who are you?" he stammered.

"I am Mother Earth," She said.

As He looked over Her topography, He began to feel an urge that had never been felt before. With lusty energy and divine reverence, Father Sky and Mother Earth made love for six glorious days, and as They erupted into one final surge of passion, the Universe was born. And this, my children, is what scientists have come to call the "Big Bang Theory."

• • •

Dear Swami:

Can you tell me the difference between wisdom and knowledge?

Juan Tuno,
El Paso, Texas

Dear Juan:

Knowledge is knowing. Wisdom is knowing and not saying.

• • •

Dear Swami:

I have heard many so-called "new age" gurus insinuate that we are all manifestations of God. All of my prior religious training teaches that we human beings are sinners who can only be saved by God's grace. I just don't see how we imperfect humans can all of a sudden claim to be expressing God? This idea of human divinity is sacrilegious.

Misty Mark,
Charlotte, North Carolina

Dear Misty:

You have reasoned yourself into what is known in theology as a "cul-de-sacrilege." And this is understandable because in spiritual matters, linear reasoning always ends up at a dead end. But if we try circular logic for a change, and view life as a wheel, with God as the hub and each of us as a spoke, it is easy to see how we are spokespersons for the Universal.

• • •

Dear Swami:

I know this is an oldie, but here goes: Can God make a stone so heavy He cannot lift it?

Campy Dunn,
Bloomington, Illinois

Dear Campy:

Of course He can. How do you think isometric exercise got started?

• • •

Dear Swami:

Does enlightenment come all at once? Is there a moment when we "get it?" Or is it a process of becoming more and more all the time?

Theo Rettig-Lee,
Cambridge, Massachusetts

Dear Theo:

Some people experience becoming more and more all the time, but they don't call it enlightenment—they call it gaining weight. Actually, anytime we talk about enlightenment it is clear proof we are not enlightened. Because enlightenment means being in the Now. As soon as we observe, "Oh, wow. I'm in the Now," it's too late. It's already Then. Only an inscrutable puzzle that trips the mind and causes it to stumble and lag behind the rest of our being can bring that temporary state of enlightenment. It may be too late for us, but we can definitely help our children achieve this enlightened state. Next time you are on a trip and your child asks, "Are we there yet?" say "No, we are still here." The glazed look on the child's face will be proof that enlightening has struck.

• • •

Dear Swami:

How do you feel about sage-burning for purification purposes?

Al Lurgic,
King-of-Prussia, Pennsylvania

Dear Al:

True, there are some today who would like to restore that medieval practice, but I think it would be counter-productive. Sages have always been an endangered species and particularly these days, we need every sage we can get!

• • •

Dear Swami:

How many Pop-tarts does it take to fill the Universe?

Waylon Wall,
Jerusalem, Indiana

Dear Waylon:

Pop-Tarts alone will not do the trick. If you really want to fill the Universe, you will need both Pop-Tarts and Mom-Tarts.

~~~~~~ *2* ~~~~~~

Everything You Always Wanted to Know About Sects

Are enlightened beings meant to have sects? Or can sects actually stunt our spiritual growth, not to mention endanger our health? With the recent concern about Oughtism—a highly contagious disease known to be transmitted through sects—many metaphysicians wonder whether the safest sects would be no sects at all. Swami doesn't agree. Sects between consenting adults is just fine as long as you're not obsessed with it. And it's pretty easy to tell when someone's obsessed. You see these people proselytizing door-to-door or selling flowers on the street or shooting at those whose sects preference is different from their own—one look in their eyes will tell you they'll do anything for sects. And let's face it, unbridled sects can lead to unwanted misconceptions, and goodness knows we already have enough of these in the world. So if you're going to engage in sects, I suggest you wear a protective sheath of white light. And no matter how ecstatic you get, keep your eyes open, okay?

• • •

Dear Swami:

I've spent years following various gurus, and just recently I came to the realization that I have relied on one guru or another to make all of my life's decisions for me. Now that I see how co-dependent I've been, I'm wondering if there's a support group for people like myself.

Alma B. Leaver,
Santa Barbara, California

Dear Alma:

*It is a good thing that people like you are becoming aware of your co-dependency and looking for groups to join. And I'm sure there are many more co-dependent people who would go to one of these groups, if only they could find someone to go with. At any rate, I've got good news for you. There's a new support group specifically for people who've spent too many years sitting at the feet of gurus—**Odoreaters Anonymous.***

• • •

Dear Swami:

I live down south, and as someone who believes in reincarnation, I find it difficult to find like-minded folks. Any suggestions?

Ronnie Noes,
Moultrie, Georgia

Dear Ronnie:

*You're in luck! There's a group I've heard of down in Georgia called the **Dixie Reincarnationist Church.** Now these are some real "born again" types, but they're also pretty down home. For their last rites, they say, "Y'all come back real soon now, y' heah?"*

• • •

Dear Swami:

I'm overweight, and that's how I like it. Except in this society where everyone's so hung up on being thin, fat people are shunned as if gaining weight is contagious or something. Do you know of any group that appreciates us overweight folks?

Ella Funt,
Fondue Lake, Wisconsin

Dear Ella:

Yes. You'll be happy to know that there is now an organization which actually looks upon overweight people as an elite. The group is called **Immensa,** *and only those weighing over 300 pounds are allowed to join. Called a "true mass movement" by its founders,* **Immensa** *exhorts members to "Be all that you can be—and more." Says the* **Immensa** *brochure:*

"We are put on this planet to grow, yet so few of us reach our fullest potential. Sure, spiritual growth is great but any true gains on the spiritual planes must be reflected on the physical as well. Granted, Gandhi may have been a spiritual heavyweight, but physically? If only he had gained 20 pounds, he could have been a 97-pound weakling. Such a huge aura, and only a small fraction of it occupied by form. What a pity! At Immensa, we believe in manifest destiny, that a person isn't fully actualized until his entire auric energy field is filled with physical form."

But I should warn you, there is a bit of a dark side to this organization as well. Monthly weigh-ins are held, and those unfortunates who have lost weight must go to **Confection,** *where they are stuffed with sweets and are told, "Go, and thin no more."*

• • •

Dear Swami:

Call me old-fashioned, but I just hate to wear clothes. The way I figure it, if God had meant for us to wear clothes, then He would have made Christian Dior or Levi Strauss the first man instead of Adam. Needless to say, I've had a hard time finding a religious group that would accept me as the Creator made me. Any ideas?

Abba Riginal,
Malibu, California

Dear Abba:

*It's certainly astounding how clothes-minded religions can be, isn't it? Well, I've got some good news for you. There's an obscure yet ancient sect which shares your belief, followers of the prophet **Nuddha** who traveled widely through the East—mostly in the summertime—teaching the principles of **Nuddhism**. In the beginning, he says, was the "Naked Truth." All was peaceful until people began decorating their bodies with various forms of clothing, armor, ceremonial garb—and the more people had on, the better they felt about themselves. In fact, many anthropologists believe this was the origin of the word "moron." Nuddhists who traveled from village to village had less on than just about anyone else, so their teachings were call "less-ons." And in a world where the morons have greatly outnumbered the lessons, maybe this is a religion whose time has come.*

• • •

Dear Swami:

I've been hearing a lot lately about "New Thought." What exactly is New Thought, and how does it differ from Old Thought?

Lynn Guini,
Hartford, Connecticut

Dear Lynn:

*The Old Thought governing belief is: **Bread always falls buttered side down.** New Thought maintains that bread always falls buttered side **up,** and if by some quirk your bread falls buttered side down, you obviously buttered the wrong side.*

• • •

Dear Swami:

I notice that many spiritual teachers lead excursions to sacred spots on the planet. Do you ever do this, and if so what kind of trips do you lead?

Juana Sakitumi,
San Francisco, California

Dear Juana:

Yes, as a matter of fact I do. And you're just in time to sign up for my Gobi Desert Experience. That's where I drop you off at this famous site and say, "Okay, now Gobi Desert for a week." Later on, to follow up, you might want to gobi mountain or gobi ocean. Believe me, by totally immersing yourself in the Earth's magnificence like this you can leave this training and gobi anything you want to be.

• • •

Dear Swami:

There are many different kinds of yoga, and I have tried most of them. Which yoga, in your opinion, brings greatest fulfillment?

Amir Ladd,
Maui, Hawaii

Dear Amir:

*Yes, it is true. Many go from one kind of yoga to another seeking greener postures. But to me, the most powerful form of yoga is **karma yoga**—the doing for others. And that is why so many on the path today want to be healers. And these healers tend to gather in the great power spots—like Boulder, Sedona, and of course, Hawaii. But this presents a problem for the healers because places like Hawaii are naturally healing. I* mean, the laying on of hands is nothing when compared with the handing on of leis. As a result of all this automatic healing, it makes hard for healers to make a living. That's why healers who heal well are far more plentiful than those who are well-heeled.

So for those who want to do karma yoga, it is important to identify a need and provide service towards that need. There is a very inspirational story I've heard about a young man who wanted to do karma yoga. One day, he realized that all these people on the path—did they not need a place to stay overnight? And this farsighted man has made a fortune providing lodging for seekers. Perhaps you've heard of him— Ramada Das.

· · ·

Dear Swami:

I understand you and the late Osho Rajneesh had your differences. Would you care to comment?

Imelda Trump,
Las Vegas, Nevada

Dear Imelda:

Yes, we did have some differences. For one thing, he had a beard and I do not. And he liked Rolls Royces while I prefer ascended Mazdas. But I will say one thing. If all of Rajneesh's ardent followers were laid end to end—they'd probably enjoy it immensely. But why dwell on past differences. Let's let Baghwans be Baghwans, okay?

· · ·

Dear Swami:

Can there be such a thing as addiction to Spirit? Every morning as soon as I open my eyes—before having my coffee, even— I just have to connect with the Source. Sometimes I stay in a blissful meditation for an hour or longer, and I'm late for work. Then at work, I'll sneak a quick moment of ecstatic communion with spirit when I think no one is looking—and before I know it, I've been gone for forty-five minutes. Hobbies? Relationships? Who's got time for those? Besides, anything pales when you've found The One. The problem is, I can't really relate to people and I'm on the verge of losing my job. I'm thinking of checking myself into a program, but I don't know which kind. Can you help me, Swami?

Stan Bymie,
Bliss, Missouri

Dear Stan:

With the pressures of life nowadays, it's not uncommon for folks to hit the Source a little too much, but you've got a real problem, fella. Yes, you and I both know that this is an artificial world of illusion. But what school isn't? I don't care if your Father is paying the tuition, if you flunk out you'll still have to take it over. So get high if you want to, but don't let it interfere with your studies. Some say the key to life is **karma**—*the sum total of our past actions. Others say it is* **dharma**—*our right action in the world. Me, I say it is* **drahma.** *For the world is indeed a stage, and in order for us to move on to the next stage, we must work on our act.*

• • •

Dear Swami:

One thing I have noticed is that a lot of Indian masters love to make their points by using puns. Is there some place they study where they learn to play with words like this?

Vashti Deeshes,
New York, New York

Dear Vashti:

Yes, there is. The Punjab.

• • •

Dear Swami:

I've noticed that some followers of traditional western religions seem to feel threatened by Hinduism, and even have equated yoga with "devil worship." Even in my own liberal family, when my Jewish grandmother heard I was studying yoga, she said, "Yoga? Don't you know that 'yoga' is 'a goy' spelled backward?" Is there anything that can be done to combat these misconceptions?

Haydn Sikh,
Watsonville, California

Dear Haydn:

I wish I had some good news for you, but I don't. I have heard reports that some fundamentalist Christian schools are teaching their children about an elaborate Hindu plot to use yoga, meditation, chanting, and delicious spicy food to curry favor with unsuspecting Westerners. And these curry-favoring Westerners, the story goes, will be led down the garden path until Christianity is completely co-opted by Hinduism. Allow me to quote from a pamphlet put out by Rev. Tim Tayshin's "Mortal Majority":

"Imagine, if you will, our beloved faith totally Hinduized. Imagine our young people being forced to sing krishna carols—you know, 'We Wish You A Hare Krishna' or 'Puri Roasting On An Open Fire, Kali Nipping At Your Nose', or some Elvis impersonator crooning about how 'It's gonna be a Blue Krishna without you.' But it's even more grim than that. To the tune

of 'Onward Krishna Soldiers,' our young people will become born-again, born-again, born-again Krishnas who embrace reincarnation. And here is the worst part: THOSE WHO RESIST THIS FALSE BELIEF IN REINCARNATION WILL BE FORCED TO ACCEPT IT IN THEIR NEXT LIFETIME!"

• • •

Dear Swami:

What is the origin of Sufi circle dancing?

Mae Vommitt,
Northampton, Massachusetts

Dear Mae:

Few people know this, but until the Sufis came along, the only dance was the square dance. (It's true. You can look it up.) The Sufis, being just a little lazy, decided to cut a few corners and bingo—you've got a circle dance.

• • •

Dear Swami:

I need your advice. I have been told that prayer is an extremely effective way of bringing things you want into your life—you know, "Ask and ye shall receive," and all that. Well, some people say that you must put all of your requests through on one channel—Catholicism, Buddhism, and so forth. But I have this desire to pray through all different religions. What do you think, Swami? By the way, I should tell you that I am one of your biggest fans.

Sal Vayshin,
Beacon, New York

Dear Sal:

I'm glad to hear you're such a big fan, Sal. Big fans can be very help-ful, especially in summertime. As for my advice, I'd play the percentages and use them all. It's never a good idea to put all your begs in one askit.

• • •

Dear Swami:

I have a co-worker who drives me nuts. He is one of these reli-gious fanatics who believes that every little decision in his life must be justified by a passage from the Bible. He is constantly haranguing me about how I'm gonna burn in hell if I don't live my life by the Good Book. I know he means well, but how can I get this guy to lighten up a little?

Rolf Pfing,
Minneapolis, Minnesota

Dear Rolf:

I suggest first that you acknowledge him for having the integrity to hold himelf to the high standards of the Bible. It's not everyone who would have the patience to go over every detail of his life with a Fine Couth Tome. But it is true that people with a one-tract mind like your friend tend to suffer from humorrhoids, an enlargement of the onus which makes laughter painful, if not impossible. So I recommend small doses of strained humor until he relaxes his onus a bit and allows laugh-ter to come through. I suggest you begin by testing his knowledge of the Bible. Ask him if he knows what kind of car God drives. He will look at you puzzled. You must then look at him equally puzzled and say, "I can't believe a Biblical scholar like you cannot answer this question. Everybody knows God drives a Plymouth. It's right there in Genesis—"And He drove them out of the garden in His Fury!""

• • •

Dear Swami:

In your book, *Driving Your Own Karma*, you speak about the healing power of dogs ("Teach Your Dog To Heal"). I wonder if you have any encouraging words for us cat-lovers.

> Anna Mull,
> Fair Oaks, California

Dear Anna:

Funny you should bring this up, because I have recently read about an obscure sect which believes that the most healing experience of all is the abrasive stroke of a cat's tongue. Although I myself am not a practicing member of the Catlick faith, I feel there must be something to it given how many people religiously empty litter boxes each week.

• • •

Dear Swami:

Remember the big fuss twenty-five years ago when John Lennon said the Beatles were more popular than Jesus? Well, nowadays Elvis is bigger than Jesus and nobody seems to care. I mean, do you realize that twice as many people visited the Elvis shrine at Graceland than the National Cathedral last year? And Graceland gets about ten times more in their collection plate each year than Robert Schuller does. What gives, Swami? Have we allowed some bloated, sexually perverse drug addict to unhinge us from our spiritual moorings?

> Dan Studamuzyk,
> Sterling Heights, Michigan

Dear Dan:

It is true Elvis had a checkered past (though not as checkered as Pinky Lee), but then any great spiritual master must go through earthly trials and challenges. And you can't argue with success. Presleyterianism is the fastest growing religion in the western world, and if we look a little closer we can see why. First of all, his music was the first to fully unify all the chakras. Elvis's shaking hips shook the foundations of Puritanism, and yet his terrific haircut focused everyone's attention on a higher level. And look at the elegant simplicity of the three tenets of the Presleyterian faith:

1. Love Me Tender.

2. Don't Be Cruel.

3. Please Surrender.

So when those Elvis's Witnesses come to your door next weekend and ask with sincerity, *"Are You Lonesome Tonight?"* don't be surprised if you throw up your hands and say, *"It's Now Or Never,"* and buy that ticket to Graceland.

• • •

Dear Swami:

I just read a wonderful book on meditation by the Buddhist monk Thich Nhat Hanh where he compares the process of meditation to particles in a glass of unfiltered apple juice slowly settling to the bottom. Any thoughts on this analogy?

Candyce B. True,
Fairfield, Connecticut

Dear Candyce:

My sediments exactly.

• • •

Dear Swami:

I'm sick and tired of you so-called "new age" types undermining the real religion and the things that made this country great—God, Guns and Guts. Jesus is coming, and when He does He'll be walking with us, not you.

Evan Jellick,
Lynchburg, Virginia

Dear Evan:

Since this is a Universe of infinite possibilities, you <u>may</u> be right. Now I probably have an even wilder imagination than you do, but somehow I can't see Jesus coming all the way down here just to hang out with Jimmy and Jerry and renew his membership in the National Rifle Association.

• • •

Dear Swami:

What is your theological position on chocolate? My minister tells me that chocolate is an insidious evil that causes addiction, dissolution and decay. And yet, when I bite into a chunk of my favorite sweet treat, I am filled with such ecstatic delight that I know for certain God exists. Should I pursue the chocolate path or is the road to hell indeed paved with Chunkies?

Cara Zmatick,
Grand Rapids, Michigan

Dear Cara:

*It is true that some strict fundamentalists insist that chocolate is "the Devil's Food" and that the spiritually pure should only indulge in angelfood. Personally, I feel these people are just afraid to face the dark side. Actually, chocolate worship dates back to beginning of recorded history. According to those ancient scrolls, the Tut Sea Rolls, the Egyptians worshipped cocoa as the Supreme Bean and the first pyramids were pocket-sized and made of chocolate. Modern day chocolytes include the **Goobers**, who seek to experience Almond Joy by immersing themselves in vats of hot chocolate; the **Raisonettes**, who worship* chocolate Santas mounted on their dashboards; and the **Salivation Army,** who selflessly distribute chocolate kisses to the homeless. I am all in favor of celebrating chocolate and other pleasures of life's as manifestation of spirit, and I look forward to a time in the near future when the new religious rallying cry is, *"Jesus savors!"*

• • •

Dear Swami:

I've heard that you actually have the ability to walk on water. Not only that, but you say you can teach others to do this as well. Where can I sign up?

Amin Bizniz,
Rockville, Maryland

Dear Amin:

You heard right. Like anything else in life, walking on water is quite simple as long as the conditions are right and your timing is impeccable. So I invite all of you to join me for my annual Water Walking Ceremony on Lake Minnetonka, Minnesota this January 15th. Success is virtually guaranteed.

• • •

Dear Swami:

I read somewhere that you grew up in a Methodist family. Is that true?

Rich Ewell and Sara Mony,
Rochester, New York

Dear Rich and Sara:

Actually, my father was Methodist and my mother was Catholic. So technically, I'm a Rhythm Methodist.

• • •

Dear Swami:

Was Eve really tempted by a snake? If so, what implications does this have in our present existence?

Diane Goetuhevn,
Zeeland, Michigan

Dear Diane:

I wish I could give you a definitive answer on this, but the exact circumstances of Eve's temptation are something that Biblical scholars have been disagreeing about for centuries. Fortunately, some Religious Science practitioners recently conducted a scientific experiment to determine once and for all the likelihood that Eve was actually tempted by a snake. They took a group of 500 randomly-selected people from all religions and all walks of life. In front of each person, they placed two bowls. The first had honey-vanilla-walnut ice cream smothered in rich dark chocolate fudge. The second had a snake. ninety-nine point eight percent of the group found the ice cream more tempting. (The only one who actually chose the snake was a Bushman who mistook the fudge sundae for water buffalo droppings.) From their collected data, the researchers drew three possible conclusions:

1. Eve was on a diet at the time.

2. She had kinky tastes.

3. The press agent for the Bible juiced up the story to sell more Bibles.

As for the implications, I would say, "Beware of snakes bearing gifts. Beware of salesmen bearing Bibles. Beware of Bible salesmen bearing snakes. And be particularly wary of snakes bearing hot fudge sundaes."

• • •

Dear Swami:

For years now, the channeled entity Ramtha has been giving advice. Do you, Swami, have any advice for Ramtha?

Saul Atair,
Redmond, Washington

Dear Saul:

I sure do. Hey, Ramtha. Get a life!

$$\sim\!\sim\!\sim\!\sim\!\sim\!\sim\!\sim\!\sim\!\sim\!\sim\; 3 \;\sim\!\sim\!\sim\!\sim\!\sim\!\sim\!\sim\!\sim\!\sim$$

There's No Business Like Grow Business or Two Sarongs Don't Make a Rite

All my adult life, I have been a supporter of the Human Potential Movement. Call me a cockeyed optimist, but no matter how bad the six o'clock news gets, I still think we have the potential to be human. Though it's true that for most people personal growth is something that happens between Thanksgiving and New Year's and can best be measured on a bathroom scale, more and more people are exploring the frontiers of the human mind (and the back tiers, too). And the great profusion of paths to choose from nowadays can cause terrible confusion. In fact, I've heard there's a new product for people who are so desperate to find the right spiritual path that they've become pathological. It's called Right God spray.

• • •

Dear Swami:

I've been hearing a lot lately about the power of visualization to manifest more of what you want in life. It seems pretty amazing that I can sit in my room, focus my mind and imagine something—and then have it come about. Can anyone learn to do this? And does it really work?

Lil Bitmore,
Asheville, North Carolina

Dear Lil:

Yes, it is true. Visualization is indeed a powerful tool. And unless you suffer from a serious yearning disability, it is fairly easy to do. Does it work? Absolutely! I'll give you an example. Recently, the organizer of one of my personal appearances used this technique as a major form of promotion. Each morning for two weeks, this person would meditate for half an hour and imagine a full house for the concert. And each day, the visualization became more and more vivid. Finally, the evening of the engagement arrived, and it was apparent that this imagining technique worked exquisitely. The concert hall was filled with imaginary people.

• • •

Dear Swami:

I came from a terribly dysfunctional family, and I'm afraid my whole life has been messed up because of it. When I was growing up, we never had any money. Worse than that, though, there was no laughter, joy or play. Dancing was prohibited, as was chocolate. We weren't even allowed to watch "Candid Camera" on TV. The house we lived in was horrible and always seemed to bring gloom and bad luck. About the only thing positive I can say about my parents was that they made love on a regular basis. Swami, what can I do to heal that sad inner child and turn my life around?

Furwood Flye,
Huntington, W. Virginia

Dear Furwood:

Sounds to me that your family was worse than dysfunctional. It was dysfundsional, dysfuntional, dysfunksional, dysfudgesional, dysFuntsional and even dysfengshuinal. I tell you, it's a good thing your parents had a good sex life, otherwise this answer would be unprintable. Fortunately, there is something that can be done. Vow to spend at least one day a week being a Big Brother to your inner child. Tell him you're a secret visitor from the future who has come to take him on a weekly play adventure. Do whatever he wants to do. Sure, you might look funny running around the playground with an invisible kid, but do you think your inner child cares that he's running around the playground with an invisible adult? Of course not. Then you can go out for a hot fudge sundae, watch comedy movies, or even teach the kid break-dancing.

One more thing: If you can, do both of yourselves a favor and get a dog. Go to the humane society one Saturday and pick yourselves out a puppy who is so overflowing with unconditional love that it is literally dripping over the sides of his mouth. In fact, scientists know that doggy drool contains a magical healing formula called Love Potion #K-9. And don't forget that any time we come into contact with a friendly dog, our bodies produce these hormones called "puptides" which make us feel loved and nurtured. As you cuddle that dog, imagine your inner child being nuzzled as well. Before long, you will find that the present you and your inner child have shared will be the most valuable gift either of you has ever received. As you have healed his past, so he will heal your future.

• • •

Dear Swami:

My girlfriend and I recently returned from a trip to Tahiti. While we were there, we tried on these beautiful sarongs and both of us had the same amazing experience. Instantly, we were transported back to a lifetime where we were Tahitian priestesses performing sacred rites. Words and chants seemed to flow through us while we wore these enchanting outfits. Needless to say, we bought them and planned to use them in a ritual celebration when we got back to the states. We invited all of our friends to the ceremony. They sat around in a large circle, my friend and I came in wearing our sarongs and we waited for the magical words to come out of our mouths—and nothing happened. It was so-o-o embarrassing! Our friends left puzzled and we were left wondering what went wrong. Swami, did we violate some great Universal law?

Hedda Vertyme,
Topanga Canyon, California

Dear Hedda:

Yes, I'm afraid you did. Two sarongs don't make a rite.

• • •

Dear Swami:

For years now, I've been waiting for my soulmate to show up and frankly, I'm growing impatient. It isn't that I've been passively waiting either. I've done affirmations, visualizations, ceremonies and meditations. I've had Science of Mind practitioners do "treatments" for me, all to no avail. I'm beginning to think that this "mind science" stuff just doesn't work. What do you think?

Rosa Krewshin,
Houston, Texas

Dear Rosa:

Oh it works all right, but you have just stumbled into the major pitfall in using infinite powers to "get" things on earth. You are trying to set linear rules for the Infinite, and that's like trying to steer a 747 with a buggywhip. As far as the Universe is concerned, it's always Now—so you already have everything you desire. The problem is attracting it into your linear, finite time-frame. The Universe is a fickle type, and has no patience for folks who are impatient. Therefore, the best way to make yourself attractive to Infinite Intelligence is by getting a faith-lift. Have faith, then let it go. Remember you can be happy even if your soulmate never finds you. Science of Mind is great for planting the seeds, but for true happiness nothing beats the Science of I-Don't-Mind.

• • •

Dear Swami:

A couple of years ago the great mime Marcel Marceau came to town and did a workshop to train others in the art. At first I thought it was a great idea, but that was before our town became overrun with mimes of all ages and sexes. You can't go downtown or walk around in a shopping mall without being accosted by some black-clad, white-faced ectomorph with a saccharine half-smile trying to escape from an imaginary room. I keep thinking they're going to hit me up for money or a contribution to something, but they never do, and that's what drives me absolutely nuts. I mean, what's their game, anyway? And the worst thing is, they never say anything. What are they really thinking? I have a feeling that we'd all be in big trouble if they ever escaped from those imaginary rooms. When I close my eyes to go to sleep at night, what do I see? Mimes, that's what! Mimes taunting and teasing me. Last night, I had this horrible dream in which I actually took a gun and wasted one of them. Please, Swami, I need your help before I become a tabloid headline and a (posthumous) subject for "48 Hours."

Don Crossme,
Ann Arbor, Michigan

Dear Don:

Strangely enough, I can relate to your unusual affliction. Years ago, during my hamburger days (I didn't learn about salad until I could afford steak), I had a job working for the United Mimeworkers Union. Each day, they would come in, smile, say nothing, and climb imaginary walls. I, too,

55

would be climbing walls. I took it very personally that I was getting the silent treatment. Fortunately, the union secretary, Sylvia, noticed my distress and gave me some advice. "Listen," she said, "mimes should be our worst problem. Pollution, you close your eyes, does it go away? You should live so long. War, poverty, ignorance—you close your eyes to them, and they get worse. But a mime? You close your eyes, and poof— he's gone. You know what my philosophy is? Out of sight, out of mime."

I was so impressed that I signed up for a twelve-week course in Sylvia's Mime Control. It was there that I actually grew to love being in the presence of mimes because the silence was so soothing. So I wish that you too gain peace of mime before it's too late. And for goodness sake, put that gun away. A mime is a terrible thing to waste.

• • •

Dear Swami:

Since so many folks in the personal growth field are "coming out of the closet," so to speak, about their personal battles with drugs and alcohol, I wonder if you would be willing to share something about your own background. Swami, have you ever been involved with drugs or alcohol?

Jessup DeStreet,
Biloxi, Mississippi

Dear Jessup:

I must confess that during my early years, drugs were as much a part of my life as "I Love Lucy", the World Series and birthday cake. I tried 'em all. It all started with Bayer children's aspirin then I experimented with Pepto-Bismol and Kaopectate, riding my intestinal tract like it was the Cyclone at Six Flags—and then finally the ultimate buzz, Vicks VapoRub. And I inhaled. Wow. My head still rings from that one. Fortunately, I checked myself into a good herbal cleansing program before I got onto the harder stuff, like Preparation H.

As for alcohol, I grew up in a dry county in Oklahoma and I didn't have much experience with it. In fact, the first time I heard of Southern Comfort, I thought it was a hemorrhoid remedy. (I must have gotten it mixed up with Duncan Hines.) For a short while, I did experiment with strong drink. But soon after that I came under the influence of the famous Prohibitionist, Bruno Beer. He helped me find a job with the Farmer's Union (the E.I.E.I.O.) counting Oklahoma's dairy cow population, and I haven't touched a drop since. Once a teat-totaller, always a teat-totaller I guess.

• • •

Dear Swami:

How do I handle a boss who gives me no instructions for a particular project, and then complains about how it was done? His standard reply to any request for assistance or any comment on being treated unfairly is, "That's your problem." Since I'm not in a position to look for another job, he's right. It is my problem. I even bought one of those voodoo dolls and am thinking of putting his name on it and sticking pins in strategic places. Any ideas?

Mandy Torpedos,
Berwyn, Illinois

Dear Mandy:

Please, please, please, no violence! Violence never works (unless, of course, you're a nation-state with a powerful air force). No, your boss needs your compassionate help. From what you say, it sounds like he is in the advanced stages of **assaholism.** The main symptom of assaholism is assaholic behavior—accompanied by the denial that there is any assahole problem whatsoever. It is very important that you handle this situation delicately and discreetly. Perhaps you can introduce him to a friend of yours who is a recovering assaholic, or even anonymously leave literature around about **Assaholics Anonymous.** Above all, never become self-righteous. An assholier-than-thou attitude will defeat your purpose.

• • •

Dear Swami:

I've been hearing for years about the value of just relaxing, letting go, and going with the flow. I know it's important, and yet every time I'm ready to step out on Faith, the part of me that wants to control steps in and makes a mess of things. I'm at my wits' end, Swami. If I don't learn how to surrender soon, I'm afraid I'll just have to give up. Can you help me, please?

Meg Lomania,
Toronto, Ontario

Dear Meg:

You know, I particularly relate to your situation because I've been there myself. It was in my younger days when I was still single. I, too, tried stepping out on Faith. Unfortunately, Faith found out I was stepping out on her, and she gave me my unconditional release. Despondent and unable to let go of the relationship, I went to see my guru, Harry Cohen Baba, the Garment Center Saint, who told me this heartwarming story of surrender:

Once upon a time in India, a holy man encountered a tiger in the jungle. The holy man could tell by the tiger's bony ribs that he had not eaten in many days. He also knew that a man his age could never outrun a tiger. So in complete surrender, the old man dropped to his knees, bowed his head, and began to pray. To his amazement, the tiger sat beside him and bowed his head as well.

The holy man, tears in his eyes, looked skyward and cried, "Oh, it is indeed a miracle!"

Whereupon the tiger also looked up and said, "S-s-sh! I'm trying to say grace."

• • •

Dear Swami:

I've always been the worrying kind. You name it, I've lost sleep over it. Sure, I've worried about the usual stuff—school, money, relationships, health. But I worry about other things as well—like the environment. (Back when James Watt was Secretary of the Interior, I was the one who came out with those "Watt? Me Worry!" bumper stickers.) And tidal waves. Now I live here in Oregon and there hasn't been a tidal wave here in all of recorded history—and that has me worried. It seems we're long overdue. Then there are those eerie mornings when I wake up without a care in the world. And that's when I really start to worry because I figure I'm gonna be socked with something so unimaginably bad that I haven't been able to think of it yet. Now don't get me wrong. It's not worrying that I mind. In fact, I kind of like it. Gives me something to do. But I'm worried there might be something wrong with me for worrying so much. Any advice?

Fess Supp,
Springfield, Oregon

Dear Fess:

*Sounds like you need my **Peaceful Worrier** training, where you learn to worry to your heart's content—and never let it bother you. See, worrying should be no cause for concern. It's a natural human emotion. So relax. Ninety percent of the things you worry about will never happen anyway, and the ten percent that do happen will keep you so busy, you won't have time to worry. That's why it's important to enjoy your worrying while you can.*

In fact, your penchant for extended worry might even be considered a gift. Most people would give anything to have someone to do all their worrying for them. If you charged for this service, believe me, it would eliminate your money worries anyway. I suggest you take on other people's worries, forget about your own, and make a comfortable living as a mercenary worrier.

• • •

Dear Swami:

Recent articles have called into question the authenticity of books such as *Jaguar Woman*. How about it, Swami? Your frank opinion on this—is it fact or fiction?

Jason Rabbitz,
Huntington Beach, California

Dear Jason:

I don't know about that book, but I have heard that there is a soon-to-be-released sequel which is definitely authentic. It's called BWM Woman.

• • •

Dear Swami:

I have a puzzling problem. I commute to work as part of a van pool from New Jersey to New York City. I'm just fine until we approach the Holland Tunnel, at which point I go into a severe panic. I break into a cold sweat, my breathing becomes labored, and I'm in a state of terror until we come out the other side. This only happens when someone else is driving. Can you shed any light on the situation?

Tess Driver,
Nutley, New Jersey

Dear Tess:

You are undoubtably suffering from what is known as "Carpool Tunnel Syndrome." That is when fear of not being in control severely limits your range of emotion. Sure we're driving our own karma, but what fun would it be if we could see the road ahead before we got there? Why bother making the trip? If we knew for certain where we were going, we could just sit at home and watch pre-runs. The one thing in life that is certain is Uncertainty. (And to show you how pervasive this principle is, I can't even say for sure that it's true.) So the only cure I know for Carpool Tunnel Syndrome is to relax with that Uncertainty, snuggle up to it, give it a peck on the cheek—and whenever you feel that the Universe is just too contrary to understand, you can take comfort in knowing that God loves you—even if He's not ready to make a commitment.

• • •

Dear Swami:

I like New Age music as much as the next guy, but enough is enough. There is such a thing as too relaxing. At least couch potatoes have to flick the remote once in a while. But now with automatic reverse, "massage-table potatoes" don't ever have to touch down. How about those of us who want to do something other than be? Isn't there some spiritual, uplifting music we can dance to?

Ray Zdarouf,
Royal Oak, Michigan

Dear Ray:

There's good news for all you spiritual folks who want to get off your astral and boogie down—Sufi music. In fact, there's a new CD just released on Akashic records called Sufi Safari, and it contains such hits as "Sufi U.S.A.", "Sufi Girl", "Wake Up Little Sufi" and "The Way We Whir", all recorded of course by the Four Tops. I suggest you give it a spin.

• • •

Dear Swami:

I've heard it said that there are two kinds of people in the world—those concerned with doing, and those focused on being. Can you comment?

Hy Feiber,
Tamarac, Florida

Dear Hy:

*Actually, there **are** two kinds of people in the world—those who divide people into two kinds and those who do not. Since we both seem to be the former, I will proceed to answer your question. Actually, doing and being need to be balanced in each and every one of us. Being is the inner, doing the outer. When they are out of balance, it is obvious. Like the inner-focused person who spends so much time minding his own isness, that he never has time to live his life. While it is true the unexamined life is not worth living, it is even more true that the unlived life is not worth examining.*

And then there's the other extreme, the person whose entire existence is do, do, do—and then one day he wakes up and realize his whole life has become doo-doo. So each of us must find that balance. That is why so many people who are around doers all day can't wait to come home and relax with a couple of beers.

• • •

Dear Swami:

All my life I have worried about what people will think about me. As a result, I have always been a "pleaser." Whatever people have asked of me, I have done and I've listened to and acted upon every bit of advice I've ever received. Recently someone suggested that I just be myself. That sounds good, but I just don't know how. Do you have any advice for me?

Cody Pendant
El Centro, California

Dear Cody:

Ah, yes. You have been suffering from that dreaded disease, **Oughtism.** *That is where you do what everyone says you oughta, until your whole existence becomes following oughtas. Well, it's time you stopped letting people oughta you around! Seems to me that Oughtism has you in an advice-grip that is keeping you from enjoying life. So I will indulge in your advice vice on one condition—that you promise not to follow it. Okay? First of all, I would get rid of that ridiculous idea that you have to be yourself. It is so limiting. I suggest you be someone else. Be someone new every day. Try spending a week as Elvis. Or as the Pope. Or Madonna (either one). Once you've tried all these personalities for size, pick out the parts that fit. Now I understand there's a hospital down in Houston that has started to do personality transplants, but what if your body rejects it? No, it is much better to grow your own. Be sure to pick a personality that you enjoy. And if you're worried about what other people think, I've got good news for you. Most people don't think.*

• • •

Dear Swami:

I've signed up for a fire-walking seminar next month, and I'm having second thoughts. Is there anything I can do to make sure I don't burn my feet?

Frieda Mind,
Riverside, California

Dear Frieda:

I can understand your concern. It is not uncommon for firewalking candidates to get coaled feet. To avoid this situation, I offer one sure-fire solution: Walk on your hands.

• • •

Dear Swami:

I know judging and blaming just aren't appropriate in the new age, but I'm wondering how to respond when I think someone is being an inconsiderate jerk.

Mel LoFello,
Aptos, California

Dear Mel:

It is simple. Remember, it is we who create our own reality (even though a lot of reality is now made in Taiwan because of cheaper labor). So don't ever tell another human being he or she is an inconsiderate jerk. Take responsibility. Say, "Why did I create an inconsiderate jerk like you in my life?"

• • •

Dear Swami:

I have a terrible self-esteem problem. I feel tremendously insignificant, as if no one knows or cares I exist. Some people feel alienated because they feel like a number. Well, I feel like a "zero." I'm tired of feeling like a nobody! Isn't there someone who can help me? I'd sign my name, but nobody would recognize it anyway, so why bother?

Anonymous,
Somewhere, U.S.A.

Dear Anonymous:

Whoever you are, I've got some good news for you and some bad news. The good news is that there's a new self-help organization for people just like you called Anonymous Anonymous. The bad news is, they have an unlisted number.

• • •

Dear Swami:

I know you're one of those Pollyanna positive-thinking types and I have to tell you that the only true path through life is to accept and embrace the misery and tragedy. My secret for successful living is: Expect to be miserable! That way, if it happens, there's no surprise. And if it doesn't, well there's a brief respite. What do you think?

Ty Tass,
Somerset, New Jersey

Dear Ty:

Hey, whatever makes you happy.

• • •

Dear Swami:

I'm approaching retirement age, and frankly the thought of retiring bores me. It's not that I love my job that much. It's just—well, what would I do if I had to be at home all the time? This all seems so ridiculous because I've spent the last forty-five years working so that I can retire, and now I dread it. Any ideas?

Sammy Conchas,
Burbank, California

Dear Sammy:

Sure. First of all, forget retiring. Retiring is an obsolete concept that has no place in this Age of Awakening we are entering. Think about it. All throughout your work life, you've probably been tiring. And now that your work life is nearly over, you want to re-tire? What for? You've already done that. Tell them you're so tired of tiring you never want to do it again. Say you're re-awakening instead, and see if that doesn't run a little more current through the old circuits.

• • •

Dear Swami:

Lately, I've been waking up feeling listless. This is particularly frustrating because I have so much to do. The doctors can find no physical problem, yet I can't seem to muster the energy to do all those things I should. How can I get rid of this listlessness?

Kay Ottick,
Edmonton, Alberta

Dear Kay:

*Actually, you **should** be cultivating listlessness. Sounds like you have too many lists in your life already, and that is what is exhausting you. I suggest giving yourself two days a week to totally ignore all of your lists. You should have only one item on your To Do list on those days: BE LIST-LESS! Don't plan a thing. You'll be delighted at how enjoyable that listless feeling can be. Remember, a little listing is normal as you sail through life—but list too much and you'll capsize.*

• • •

Dear Swami:

I am troubled by constant guilt. You name it, I feel guilty about it. The national debt? I went out and got a second job just to help pay it off. Because there are children starving in Africa, I feel guilty if I don't finish everything on my plate. So now I weigh 325 pounds—and they're still starving. And on those rare days when I wake up and don't feel guilty, that's when I end up feeling guilty for not feeling guilty. I think this must be a hereditary condition I got from my mother. Isn't there some kind of drug that can help me?

Hyman Sain,
Roslyn, New York

Dear Hyman:

Yes, there is. The drug is called Deniasin, and it was popularized by Col. Oliver North. The drug dissolves guilt in minutes and leaves no unpleasant aftertaste—except in those who do not swallow it.

• • •

Dear Swami:

Maybe I should be addressing this question to Miss Manners, but I know you'll know what I'm talking about. Why is it that apparently well-meaning people will come over and give you bone-crushing hugs and think they're being "loving?" Sometimes I return from a workshop or other personal growth-type event feeling like a tube of toothpaste that's been squeezed in the middle. Is there anything I can do to keep from being bear-hugged to death?

Ida Klein,
Ft. Lauderdale, Florida

Dear Ida:

I'm afraid that at the present time nothing can be done legally, since the Constitution protects the right to bear arms. However I have it on good authority that a comprehensive Arms Control bill is now in Congress which would allow no hugging without full consent of the huggee. Violators would be required to attend Hug Abuse Clinics where

67

ostensibly they would learn the difference between a hug and the Heimlich Maneuver. Meanwhile, I suggest a couple of ways to avoid being a hugging victim. One, I call the "defensive hug." When you see someone who might be of the species Neanderthalus Crushyoursternum heading in your direction, boldly walk up to them and pin their arms by hugging them yourself. Then smile and disengage before they can hug you back. In extreme cases, I would recommend mace, although a lit cigarette or (especially) cigar sticking out of your mouth should repel even the most persistent huggers. If all else fails, screaming, "Help! I'm being hugged!" should cause the offensive party to disengage.

● ● ●

Dear Swami:

Although I can't really remember any details, I have this feeling that you and I were very connected in a previous lifetime. It also feels like we did a lot of traveling across great distances. Do you have any take on this?

Al Terrigo,
Camden, New Jersey

Dear Al:

I've done some interdimensional scanning, and indeed you are right. In fact, it was in a relatively recent lifetime that we were Siamese twins. We really got to work on attachment that time around. And you're absolutely right about the travel. We went back and forth each year from the U.S. to England so each of us would have a chance to drive.

● ● ●

Dear Swami:

There's a tremendous untapped potential in our society that we haven't begun to use—the power of the human mind. Specifically, I believe that each of us has undeveloped psychic power.

How about it, Swami? Do you think we will harness psychic energy for human and planetary benefit in the future?

Ray D. Onyx,
Virginia Beach, Virginia

Dear Ray:

*In a recent visit to the future, I was pleased to find that indeed psychic power was being used in all areas of life, and we were saving tremendous amounts of time and energy as a result. For example, psychic shopping will be all the rage. In fact, there will be a huge department store where all the employees will be psychic. It will be called **Seers.** Yes, as soon as you walk into the store, they will already have your order waiting for you. Or, you can do the Seers shop-by-mail program. That's where every month they ship you an item you're going to need later that month. And you'll never have to worry about overextending your budget as long as you have a Seers credit card. Most stores will approve or reject credit based on past credit ratings. Seers will base theirs on future credit ratings.*

Oh, it will be an amazing world indeed. There will be psychic advertising agencies. All they'll have to do is beam their messages to targeted mailing lists—just beaming their thoughts at the list will be enough, so they'll never have to do any actual mailing. Think of how much money this will save! Speaking of saving money, since we will already know who is going to win the elections, there will be no need for losing candidates to spend any money on debates or advertising. This is good news for people who hate missing their regular TV shows.

The psychic revolution will have a great effect on the world of sports. Instead of betting on the Sunday football game, fans will bet on the Saturday pigskin preview shows. Since only the most die-hard fans will end up watching the game itself, this will free up a lot of time for most people. The era of the overpaid athlete will give way to the era of the overpaid psychic. But we are still many years from this scenario, as we still have a long way to go in developing psychic powers. Case in point: I was recently invited to speak at a psychic fair. When I got there, I learned it had been cancelled due to unforeseen circumstances.

• • •

Dear Swami:

I'm a big fan of the actress Dianne Wiest—I loved her in *Parenthood*—and I'm also a big booster of personal growth seminars. I recently read in some tabloid that some of her friends in L.A. have been pressuring her to take the Forum, the updated version of Werner Erhard's est training. Swami, you seem to have good intuition about these things. Will she give in and take the training?

> Yolanda Playne,
> Covington, Kentucky

Dear Yolanda:

No, she won't. I'm afraid that old saying is true: "Wiest is Wiest and est is est, and never the twain shall meet."

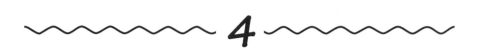

4

How to Live to Be 150—And Never Look a Day Over 100

Much has been written in recent years about the relationship between our thoughts and feelings and our physical health. Many holistic health practitioners claim that a positive mental attitude can prevent and at times even cure physical illness, while more skeptical medical authorities insist patients with a positive attitude don't really feel better—they just think they do. But I believe the most powerful organ in the immune system is the will. It stands to reason that if we harbor ill-will, we get ill. Fortunately, we can get well by being well-intentioned. Yes, I definitely believe emotions can be pre-cursors of illness. First we curse ourselves in words, then we do it physically. The malady may change, but the words are the same. The issue is always self-love. And if you don't love yourself, you'd better learn how because there is no divorce. And none of this "Till death do us part." I mean, you're stuck with you for eternity even when you leave the body. Now having this loving attitude toward ourselves probably won't affect the death rate—I expect it to remain constant at about one per person. But the difference is, we will be able to graduate to the next level without making ourselves sick worrying about whether we're going to pass. Believe me, we all pass.

• • •

Dear Swami:

I am a body-worker who has a thriving practice. And yet, I feel dissatisfied because there are so many people out there who are suffering with stress and tension and who don't even know my services are available. I'd like to do some outreach work, but I'm not sure how. Any ideas?

Yugo Teikashowa,
Tiburon, California

Dear Yugo:

*It is heartening to see someone into self-development who actually wants to do something to help the working stiff. Obviously, you haven't heard of **Feels On Wheels,** the organization dedicated to bringing healing massage to those who are hopelessly out of touch. Their philosophy is simple: "Some need to be kneaded; some need to knead to be needed. Those needing kneading are kneadless needlessly as long as we heed the need to knead the needy."*

Best of luck working with the have-knots.

• • •

Dear Swami:

I've just heard about this new kind of electromagnetic therapy which causes the cells to dilate. Is this good?

Lou Swyring,
Halifax, Nova Scotia

Dear Lou:

Well it sure beats having them die early, doesn't it?

• • •

Dear Swami:

I am bothered by absentmindedness. I forget everything. Even to write this letter, I've had to keep going back to the first sentence to remind myself what I'm talking about. What can be done about this problem I've already forgotten I have?

Wanda Ring,
Torrance, California

Dear Wanda:

There are two very simple exercises you can do to alleviate absent-mindedness. Forgetfulness, by the way, is caused primarily by weak neck muscles. See, thoughts originate in the head. When the neck muscles are weak, the thoughts can fall through the neck and down into the body, where they don't do much good. So the first exercise is to tighten the neck muscles and constrict the neck. (It's true. Back in the old days when boys had to wear ties to school, they remembered more.) Now in the beginning, until your neck muscles are really strong, there's bound to be some leakage. That's why you should stand on your head at least twice a day. This will allow the thoughts to rush back into your brain. If this doesn't work, forget it.

• • •

Dear Swami:

I have been concerned about the rising cost of health care in this country. Even with universal health insurance, there is nothing to keep down the cost. I keep thinking we could focus more on prevention, and using our mental faculties and the wisdom of the ages to stay healthier. Any thoughts on this, Swami?

Heidi Ductibal,
Milwaukee, Wisconsin

Dear Heidi:

You are definitely on the right track. Even physicians know that 80% of physical ailments get better all by themselves without any medical care. What most patients need is reassurance and an encouraging word. That's why I'm very excited about a new project being launched in Pleasantville, Iowa. It's called the **Center For Platitudinal Healing***, and here's how it works. You call their 900 number and you hear a calm, soothing, reassuring voice offering every conceivable healing platitude from "An ounce of prevention is worth a pound of cure" to "This, too, shall pass." You end up paying a small fraction of what you would if you'd gone to a doctor, not to mention siphoning off a little money from the Medical-Industrial Complex and giving it to some creative humanities students instead.*

• • •

Dear Swami:

I've tried 'em all—jogging, dance aerobics, Nautilus, and every workout tape from Jane Fonda's to Wilma Flintstone's. But somehow, there's a spiritual dimension that seems to be missing from these. Any ideas?

Mindy Yarmy,
Ft. Bragg, North Carolina

Dear Mindy:

If you're really interested in a form of physical exercise that offers a deep spiritual dimension as well, may I suggest **Bun-Sai***, the Japanese art of buttock-sculpting. You know how thorough those Japanese are— they believe in leaving no stern untoned.* **Bun-Sai** *is a very difficult and arduous path indeed, but it is perfect for those who believe the end justifies the means.*

• • •

Dear Swami:

Do you think our government will ever recognize the benefits of preventive medicine, specifically the benefits of relaxation and meditation?

Michael Ostomy,
Sarasota, Florida

Dear Michael:

I recently returned from a trip to the future, and I'm happy to report that yes, the government will take a keen interest in this kind of preventive medicine. Within a few years, it will be revealed that unmanaged stress is at the root of 80% of illness and accounts for $30 billion in medical costs annually. Under pressure from insurance companies, our government will require that all citizens take part in mandatory relaxation programs. Biofeedback devices to measure relaxation will be common at the workplace, and employees will compete fiercely for the coveted "Most Relaxed Employee Award." Nap time will become a part of the workday, but old habits will die hard as thousands of recalcitrant employees will face disciplinary action for not sleeping on the job. Workaholics will be strongly encouraged to enroll in 24-Step programs (12 steps just aren't enough of a challenge for these people), and the term "working" will itself fall into disfavor. For example, it will be considered politically incorrect for a waitperson to ask, "Are you still working on that or shall I take it away?"

On the governmental front, the Secretary of Meditation will become a cabinet-level position, and Congress will debate whether free mantras should be passed out to the Omless. Federal money will go toward developing Languish Arts programs in our high schools. Meanwhile, the government will promote meditation as a cure for many forms of mental illness, and billboards proclaiming "Get deep rest, not depressed" will be visible from every freeway in the country.

However, like many a noble battle, the War On Stress will have its casualties. Working more than twenty hours a week will become a crime, and a newly-empowered enforcement arm, the Federal Bureau of Relaxation, will offer rewards for apprehending lawbreakers who make their notorious Best-Stressed List. Ironically, the courts will be working overtime as thousands of hard-core work addicts face jail sentences for resisting a rest.

• • •

Dear Swami:

I know I need to exercise, but I'm such a couch potato that my kids got me a remote to fetch my remote because they got tired of me asking them to get it for me. Can you help me?

Ben Schwarmer,
Philadelphia, Pennsylvania

Dear Ben:

Your situation reminds me of a gentleman I knew years ago who weighed 350 pounds and spent eight hours a day doing bench presses. Unfortunately, the bench was in front of a picnic table and what he was pressing against it was his gluteus maximus. My advice to you is the same advice that worked for him:

1. START SLOWLY. Each day place your remote five feet further away. Continue to use it to mute out all commercials. After five days, you will feel a strange sensation in your body. It's called a pulse. Stay with it.

2. WORK-OUT TO WORK OUT TENSIONS. Buy a loaf of Wonder Bread and squeeze it into a pasty lump. Imagine the tension leaving your jaw, neck and shoulders and strengthening your hands and arms. If you are able to harness even a small bit of your tension, you will soon be able to change tires without a lug wrench.

3. BEGIN A PROGRESSIVE WALKING PROGRAM. *Each week, walk in a progressively more dangerous part of town. This will naturally spur you to increase your speed, until running feels more comfortable than walking.*

4. MAKE YOUR EXERCISE PROGRAM FUN. *The purpose of exercise is to keep you young, and the younger you act the younger you'll feel. Be the kind of grown-up your kid is embarrassed to be seen with. Go to the mall dressed in multi-colored spandex and run up the down escalator.*

I guarantee it—with this program, even the lumpiest couch potato will turn into a slender, sizzling French fry.

• • •

Dear Swami:

I recently read that so-called Type A people—those who are quick to anger, overly judgmental and suspicious of others, and always in a hurry—tend to be far more susceptible to heart disease than those who are more calm and understanding and less driven. Even though this sounds like something dreamed up by some wimpy humanist at one of those effete California universities, I figure it's worth checking out since so many of my co-workers have implied that I might be Type A myself. The jerks are probably jealous. But hey, I'm open-minded. And besides, my doctor just informed me that I'm a candidate for a coronary bypass, so what harm could it do to try something a little less invasive first, eh? So how about it Swami. Is it possible to heal the heart without surgery? Please put this letter at the top of your list, because if it's one thing I hate, it's waiting.

Boyle Dover,
Somerville, Massachusetts

Dear Boyle:

I appreciate your question, although I haven't been that crazy about your calls at all hours of the night asking when the hell I was going to answer your blankety-blank question and your threats to "tandoori" my hide if I didn't get on the case immediately. My goodness, if all of my correspondents were like you, I'd turn into a Harried Krishna in no time. I think your deepest problem is metaphysical—when the Lord gave out patience, you got tired of waiting in line and left. Aside from that, let me commend you on making the effort to open your heart before some surgeon does it for you. But please, slow down! Constantly being in a hurried, adrenalized state is dangerous for the heart. Truly you are playing rushin' roulette.

You've got a serious wait problem, but it's not the wait that causes heart problems, it's your attitude about your wait. If you hate to wait, you got it backwards. You should wait to hate instead. So I suggest that next time you're waiting in line at the store and you start to feel burdened by your wait, that you simply relax, take a deep breath and use the time to think about all the things in your life that you love. Do this enough, and I guarantee it will be habit-forming. Before long, you will automatically seek out the longest line.

As for the heart bypass, I suspect you've already had one. At some point, you decided to bypass your heart while making decisions about what to be in life and how to treat others. So I suggest you get off of the bypass at the very next exit, get on the main artery, and start listening to your own heart. For in your heart, there is a great Auricle whose wisdom can direct your life. What many people find when they consult the Auricle, is that they have closed their heart to people by holding onto grudges. So the next exercise I suggest is to systematically forgive everyone—including yourself and God—that you have banished from your heart, and invite 'em back in. Believe me, this Invitemin therapy works better than any bypass.

Finally, you must embrace the world. Go on a high hilltop and face the sun. Stick your arms straight out and imagine you are actually embracing the planet. (Please keep your arms above the equator until you know the world better, okay?) This is a particularly good exercise to do any time you are feeling a bit crucified, if you know what I mean. When it feels as if life has crossed you, you can double-cross the negative experience by embracing it. Do these exercises, and you truly will have a change of heart.

• • •

Dear Swami:

I understand that the Eastern European countries are way ahead of us in using the power of laughter as a healing force. Do you know anything about this?

Annette Worker,
Boulder, Colorado

Dear Annette:

What you have heard is true. In Czechoslovakian recovery rooms, for example, patients are actually hooked up to tubes and humor is interjected (in a light vein, of course). When they leave the hospital, recovering patients are instructed to take a daily laughsitive. Patient compliance isn't always what it could be, though, and it's not uncommon to see Czechs returned for insufficient funs.

• • •

Dear Swami:

I read somewhere that extremely low frequencies can cause depression. Is that true?

> Meaghan Whuppy,
> Newton, Massachusetts

Dear Meaghan:

Yes, there is some truth to that. Several years ago, a study showed that people whose frequency was once or twice a year tended to be more depressed than those whose frequency was, let's say, three times a week. But thanks to our remarkable capacity for optimism and resiliency, this need not always be true. I remember years ago meeting a man whose frequency was extremely low. And yet, I've never seen anyone happier or more aglow. I had to ask how he did it. I said, "You've just told me your frequency is once every six years, and yet you're smiling as if you're the happiest man on earth. Why is that?"

"Because tonight's the night," he replied.

• • •

Dear Swami:

As a smoker, I feel like I'm facing a great deal of judgment by nonsmokers. There's so much anti-smoking feeling nowadays, that I feel guilty lighting up in public. It used to be my friends would tell me to stop because it was bad for me. Now they tell me to stop because it is bad for them—you know, secondary smoke and all that. I've tried quitting many times, but I just haven't found a program that will help me quit once and for all. Any suggestions? And if I finally decide that I do want to be a smoker after all, how can I indulge without being guilt-tripped by my friends?

> Carson O'Gynn,
> Boylston, Massachusetts

Dear Carson:

I can certainly sympathize with you. Eliminating that nasty habit is for many a lifetime project. Like the man I read about who was facing a firing squad and was asked if he wanted a cigarette. "No thanks," he said. "I'm trying to quit." But there is hope. First off, there is a new organization that is even more effective than **Smoke Stoppers.** It's called **Butt Kickers.** If you cannot do it yourself, they come over and kick your butt for you.

And as far as guilt-tripping goes, I have even better news. I want you to think back ten or fifteen years ago when you were at the beach or at a park. Inevitably, someone with a huge, loud boom-box would show up in the vicinity and pollute everyone's air with their idea of music. And with three or four boom-boxes each playing a different tune, the air could really get foul. Then, all of that changed thanks to a simple invention— the Walkman. Now people can ingest any kind of music—no matter how toxic—and their neighbors remain unaffected (unless listeners absent-mindedly sing along with the tape). Well, if Walkman was the invention of the 80s, the invention of the 90s is . . . **Smokeman**! An attractive gas mask-type device attached to tubes and a small tank, Smokeman traps all the smoke-filled air then recycles it for continuous smoking pleasure. Preliminary tests show that Smokeman is 99.5% effective in preventing secondary smoke. Unfortunately, mass marketing is being held up by two powerful interest groups. The tobacco industry is against it because the smoke is recycled, thus fewer cigarettes are smoked. The No Smoking clinics are also against it because they say it's ruining their business. It seems that just a week or so using Smokeman, and even the most die-hard smoker is ready to quit.

• • •

Dear Swami:

This is kind of a personal question, but here goes. Do you know of any breast enlargement techniques which don't involve implants? Something simple, nontoxic and inexpensive?

Bic Parker,
Chicago, Illinois

Dear Bic:

I can see this is a very delicate issue with you because you obviously used a pen name. Anyway, your choice not to use implants is a wise one. I know of no man who wants to be with a woman who calls her cleavage "Silicon Valley." So I have a simple yet elegant solution for you, something which I recently read about. You know the folks who manufacture the pump-up bikini? Well, they now have developed a magnifying-lens bra. You can control the size of your breasts simply by changing lenses! If a very high-power lens strains the credibility, you can grow your breasts slowly by gradually strengthening the lenses. And when you're with your lover and it's time to remove the lenses, no problem. Just take them off and cry out, "Oh, no! My breasts have mysteriously shrunk and they need to be revived, quick! Do you know CPR?" Women tell me this gets amazing results.

• • •

Dear Swami:

I know I overeat, but I can't help it. Maybe it's psychological, but I get a great deal of fulfillment from food. All I have to do is sit down at the table, and I go into some sort of trance state—and I snarf up everything in sight. I'm tired of answering to the nickname, "The Prince of Whales." Can you offer any suggestions, Swami?

Stu Pendiss,
Akron, Ohio

Dear Stu:

Yes, your problems are undoubtedly psychological. You are obviously suffering from an unresolved edible complex. You think something is edible and you put it in your mouth, and boom—you gain weight. Another characteristic of the unresolved edible complex is eating until you're overfull—in other words, mistaking feeling full for feeling fulfilled. But as you yourself have pointed out, that full feeling isn't all that fulfilling. Fortunately, I have come up with a new invention that will allow you to fill your dinner plate, and still lose weight—eating glasses. Just put them on before taking your portion, and then take your normal portion of food. Since these eating glasses will be magnifying your food by 30%, you'll actually be eating 30% less! Meanwhile, I suggest you fill your plate of life with heaping portions of love, fun and service and you will never again confuse fulfillment with feelfullment.

• • •

Dear Swami:

I was just at an Expo-type event, and someone tried to sell me one of those weight-loss patches. You know: put it on and it helps you lose weight. Do those things really work?

> Faye Daway,
> Spokane, Washington

Dear Faye:

They absolutely do. Just affix one to your mouth and leave it there for about a month. You'll be amazed at the results.

• • •

Dear Swami:

I have read that taking lecithin daily actually improves the memory. Is there any truth to this?

Milton Yarmouth,
Annapolis, Maryland

Dear Milton:

Yes. According to recent studies, 75% of those people who took lecithin daily showed marked improvement in their memories. Unfortunately, only 25% of those who took part in the study could remember to take their lecithin in the first place.

• • •

Dear Swami:

I am concerned about the toxins in our air, water, soil and food. Will taking anti-oxidants help us get rid of free radicals in our system?

Aaron DeRoom,
Redondo Beach, California

Dear Aaron:

Since I am not licensed to practice medicine—in fact, I'm not even licensed to drive—I will take this question to a higher level and answer it metaphysically. As far as anti-oxidants go, they are unnecessary because it is an established metaphysical principle that there are no oxidants. Now free radicals roaming around your system can be a problem, particularly when they are having their sit-ins and demonstrations. And believe me, it is no picnic when they march on your liver and demand equal rights for viruses. Personally, the best way to deal with these free radicals is to co-opt them into the system. Have them do environmental work, like growing healthy flora in the intestines or making sure the sewage treatment facilities don't dump toxic waste into the bloodstream. Remember, like so many other entities, these free radicals are looking to be loved and useful. Behind every free radical is an inner child who is rebelling.

• • •

Dear Swami:

I realize that as part of my inward journey, I must clean and purify my physical body. I already adhere to a strict vegetarian diet. Is there anything else that you suggest doing on the physical plane to facilitate cleansing? Do you recommend colonics, for example?

Herb Biffiris,
Santa Cruz, California

Dear Herb:

Colonics? I think that is a strange place to begin the inward journey. First of all, you are going against the natural flow of things. Secondly, when you're done, all of your work goes down the tubes. I suggest that if you want to do powerful work on the physical level, try to incorporate the four elements—earth, air, fire, water—into your daily routine. I myself do this each day. I take a scalding hot bubble bath while wearing my old earth shoes. Water is especially good for you because it replaces old tissues—and you know how disgusting it can be to see those old tissues around.

• • •

Dear Swami:

Do you know anything about mercury toxicity?

Ed Nauseum,
Warren, Michigan

Dear Ed:

I don't know how toxic those Mercuries are, but I recently had a bad experience with a Ford van that I rented. Every time I got near this particular vehicle, I would get nauseated, I would get headachey and my nose would run. I finally went to an environmental toxicologist, who told me that low frequency electrical impulses from the van's radio antenna were making me sick. The situation was easily remedied by returning the van, but I don't think this Swami will ever get over the embarrassment of being told I had a van aerial disease.

• • •

Dear Swami:

I had a sports injury a while back that had me in quite a bit of pain. The doctor gave me some heavy-duty painkillers, but actually the injury never quite improved. Finally, in desperation I went to see a chiropractor. Damned if the injury didn't clear up and now I feel better than ever. Needless to say, I now get my back cracked regularly at the chiropractor's office and my doctor is wondering whatever became of me. My friends are telling me I'm deluding myself, that chiropractic can be expensive and habit-forming. They suggest I get treated by a physician instead. What do you think, Swami?

Dennis Selbow,
Yonkers, New York

Dear Dennis:

While it is true that some chiropractic patients may become "crack addicts," I find it's generally good for health and well-being to get a regular attune-up by your favorite disk jockey. It's kind of maddening how the American Medical Association has publicly disparaged the positive benefits of the chiropractic adjustments. I look forward to a time when these two groups can work together and there can be adjustice for all. Not that the medical profession is totally useless (although any system that gets 90% of its information from taking apart dead people has to be suspect). In fact, for true peace of mind during the healing process, I recommend being treated by a physician. I'm sure if doctors treated patients to ice cream, a movie, or especially a comedy club, folks would get better quicker. Our health care system seems to have it all backward. I mean, if the doctors are supposed to be doing the treating, why are the patients picking up the tab?

• • •

Dear Swami:

I have heard that you no longer experience illness on the physical plane. Is that true?

Justin Credible,
San Diego, California

Dear Justin:

I don't know how these stories get started. Actually, you are partially correct. In fact, I no longer experience physical illness, although I do catch more ethereal diseases from time to time. Right now, for example, I'm getting over a case of spiritual laryngitis. That's where you lose your inner voice.

5

How To Cure Dope Addiction and Heal the Body Politic

You know the biggest political and social problem we face today? Dope addiction. That's right. We are definitely addicted to electing dopes to public office, and these dopes are addicted to us electing them. Talk about co-dependency. I mean, look at the President and Congress trying to come up with a solution for the deficit. The President is hopelessly addicted to the popularity polls. And Congress has a campaign-fund habit that just won't quit. As soon as they get elected, they begin concentrating on their next fix. And all the money contributed by the oil and auto lobbies has made Congress truly chemically-dependent, a condition which has clouded their ability to make decisions. That is why there is all this endless arguing about the energy tax. We need mass action and what do we get instead? Mass-debating.

But we cannot blame our elected officials for our own dope addiction. Some conservatives have traced our problems to the Beatniks back in the '50s. Me, I say it's not the Beatniks that are at the root of this problem, but the Bleatniks. That is right. There are far too many sheep in this country, who follow the herd and elect leaders who pull the wool over their eyes. No wonder people felt so sheepish after Watergate. And still—the bleat goes on. So here is my modest proposal for kicking the dope habit:

1. Realize we must drive our own karma. The government is us, acting on what we perceive to be the commonweal. Since the squeaky weal gets the grease, if you want something to change you gotta squeak up. Don't let the experts tell you, "Leave the driving to us." If we want the planet to get into gear, we must make the shift ourselves.

2. Don't put yourself above politics. The only human beings who are truly "above" politics are those who are no longer walking on the Earth plane. Idealism is fine, but politics always comes down to deal-ism. So if you don't like how the deal is going down, I suggest you get out there and vote for the imperfect candidate who is most open to the environmentally-conscious, holistic, future-oriented vision we seem to share.

3. If you want a New World Order, you must fill out a New World Order Form. Even with all the talk in recent years about the New World Order, a lot of folks are saying, "Hey, no one took my order." Indeed, politicians are like waiters. They exist to take orders. While there is no doubt they pay more attention to the Big Tippers (and we're not talking about Mrs.Gore here), it is we who pay the bills that keep them in business. If you want them to fill your New World Order, you must put the order in writing. A word of caution: Be prepared for your elected servants to tell you that what you ordered is not on the menu. I'll tell you what, though. If enough of us put in the same order, they'll have to make it.

• • •

Dear Swami:

For years I've been hearing about a paradigm shift that was about to happen, but it looks to me like folks are as ignorant as ever. I've been waiting patiently, working on my own consciousness, but what about everybody else? I mean, look at what the '80s were like. How about it, Swami. Where's the beef?

Tex Tyle,
Arlington, Texas

Dear Tex:

It's true that for most people, a paradigm shift is someone giving them 20 cents to buy a newspaper. But actually, there is a major shift taking place—and we must help it along. Sure, consciousness is an asset, but we cannot just sit on our assets. We must develop and share our alternative vision. How else are we going to alter the natives? After all, the old paradigm has its missionaries. Why not us? If we're going to clear the air for the next generation, we're going to need a lot of catalytic converters—and that's where we come in. You know those churches that encourage members to picket new age events? How about picketing them and handing out flyers saying, "Is Your Planet Saved?"

And the right-to-lifers? Granted, life may begin at conception, but it certainly doesn't end at birth. So why not encourage this organization to donate half of its budget to care for some of those born fetuses who are unwanted? Now some words of caution. Since most people in this country are hung up about sects, it is very important that you not be recruiting for any group when you do your catalytic converting. Speak only for yourself. And remember that the Universe has a strange sense of humor—so there's always the possibility that they're right and you're wrong. So go forth, my children, and always remember the words of my beloved guru, Harry Cohen Baba: "Drive your karma, curb your dogma."

• • •

Dear Swami:

Here something that really drives me up the wall. How can those so-called "right-to-lifers" be so concerned with unborn fetuses and so unconcerned once those fetuses are actually born? Instead of improving the conditions of poor and unwanted children, they're perfectly content to build more prisons and spend $40,000 per prisoner per year to keep them there. How can people think this way, and is there a cure?

Osborne Poe,
Atlanta, Georgia

Dear Osborne:

I know what you mean about unwanted children. I read about someone recently who was unwanted as a child and now he's wanted in twelve states. I agree with you that too many folks in the Right-To-Life movement really belong to that other group, Right To Life Without Parole. But these people cannot take all the blame for their flawed thinking. Sadly, they are suffering from Irony Deficiency due to the irony-poor diet they were fed in school. Ironically, seeing a doctor cannot improve this condition, but seeing a paradox will. For best results, I recommend pumping ironies to increase brain mass and self-definition, fasting from TV for 30 days, and a daily enigma to release intellectual constipation.

• • •

Dear Swami:

What is your position on "political correctness?"

Felinda Blanks,
Oakland, California

Dear Felinda:

Well, there are some benefits. For example, Americans are being forced to abandon the clichés of the past and develop the clichés of the future. For example, it is no longer appropriate to call someone "fat"— they are metabolically challenged. Nor can you say someone is "dumb." That person is clue-deficient. The folks we used to call "jerks" must now be referred to as recovering assaholics. Even the term "women" (or even "womyn") has fallen into disrepute. The new term that now reflects women's enhanced political standing is Vagino-Americans, no doubt an answer to the late Lyndon Johnson's call for support from "My Phallo-Americans." Where will all this end? Probably with the invention of less insulting terms for "politically correct" and "politically incorrect." We will really have come a long way when we refer to politically incorrect people as differently sensitive, and hard-core politically correct folks as humorally impaired.

• • •

Dear Swami:

There's a lot about this last Presidential campaign that I found embarrassing, but perhaps the most embarrassing was George Bush comparing himself to former President Harry Truman. Why did he make a fool of himself by comparing himself to a Democrat that he didn't even vote for?

Lon Mohr,
Independence, Missouri

Dear Lon:

I think it has deep psychological roots and has to do with George Bush's basic insecurity about his manhood. You remember the "wimp factor?" Sure, he killed a couple of hundred thousand Iraqis and single-handedly kicked Geraldine Ferraro's behind, but still his macho image has been called into question. For example, there's been a persistent rumor in Texas that George Bush actually despises pork rinds, and secretly eats broccoli—maybe even broccoli quiche. So it was natural for President Bush to want to prove once and for all that he is indeed a Hairy True Man.

• • •

93

Dear Swami:

Like many Americans who supported President George Bush in the Persian Gulf, I am concerned that after all the destruction and bloodshed, Saddam Hussein is still in power and is still a military threat. Were we correct in going after him? And is there any way we can neutralize his threat and bring lasting peace to the area?

> Annie Mae Jerdude,
> McLean, Virginia

Dear Annie:

While I have no desire to see this despot Saddamize the Middle East, I also see we are caught between Iraq and a hard place. Even if we avoid full-scale war—the ultimate "Iraqi Horror Picture Show"—and even if we prove militarily fit, we may not be fiscally fit enough to survive another such build-up. As for going after Saddam in the first place, I can understand why we did it even though it went against all my peace-loving tendencies. But as my beloved guru Harry Cohen Baba used to say: "I think it's a terrific idea to invite the lion in to lie down with the lambs—as long as his teeth and claws are removed first."

I know many of us spiritual types were hoping and praying that Saddam would turn out to be benign, even though all the evidence pointed to malignancy. And we tried everything—meditation, prayer, visualization. We cut off Saddam's food supply, putting him on what we hoped would be a rapid Kuwait-loss program. But these non-invasive procedures simply did not work. We finally had to face the fact that surgery was necessary. Nobody likes an operation, particularly a military operation. But better this operation today than all of us having some unwanted radiation therapy a couple of years down the line.

Now, while this heroic intervention may be necessary in the short run, prevention is always the least costly medicine. As far as post-operative care goes, we must eliminate the toxic conditions which fed this malignancy in the first place. We can help by reducing our intake of oil— after all, there are far healthier substitutes. And we must help the entire area go on a low-assault regimen. Sure, using assault is an ancient habit but studies have shown that after folks do without it for a month or two, they find life tastes a lot sweeter.

To help people give up assault, it is essential that we provide them with a satisfying assault-substitute. The World Health Organization recommends megadoses of Vitamin Be One. When we are able to Be One with our enemy, we will no longer want to attack them, and this will greatly improve world health. As we heal the Be One deficiency that clouds our vision, we see that each nation is an organ, each individual a cell. It is both healthy and natural for these organs to cooperate for the greater good. The sooner we learn this, the sooner we will heal once and for all the body politic.

• • •

Dear Swami:

I voted for Bill Clinton in the hopes he could help get our economy out of the doldrums, and now I wonder if I was right. Seems like he's even more stuck than George Bush was. If he's going to get us on track, he's going to have to work more closely with Republicans. Did I make a mistake in not voting for George Bush?

Maury Zultz,
Highland Park, Illinois

Dear Maury:

At a time when we need a President with an eye toward the future, you probably voted for the right man. Shortly before the election, I did a past-life reading on George Bush—and discovered he is still living in a past life. And surely we don't need four more years of Quayle-ludes. But I think we have to be realistic about President Clinton's limitations. I mean, the guy doesn't even know how to inhale, and we expect him to fix the economy? The good news is that he is indeed working on a bi-partisan policy to make the United States competitive with Japan. He is sending Neil Bush, son of the former President, over there to start some S&L's and bring that country to its knees financially.

• • •

Dear Swami:

I am concerned about the ongoing Arab-Israeli situation. This conflict is particularly ironic because the two peoples have so much in common. Swami, what are your thoughts about bringing these warring peoples together?

Dee Pschitt,
King-of-Prussia, Pennsylvania

Dear Dee:

Yes, this is indeed a serious problem, because without peace, both religions are doomed. It would certainly be a tragedy if Islam became Was-lam and Israel became Was-real. Fortunately, there is a glimmer of hope. Actually, the entire simple solution was revealed to me in a recent dream. In the dream, the United Nations had decided to dispatch an emissary of peace to the West Bank, the one entity on the planet who could unite once and for all Muslim and Jew—Porky Pig!

Since neither Muslims nor Jews eat pork, it would point up something the two have in common. And unlike other well-meaning peace advocates who've ventured into the fray, Porky's definitely not going to get eaten alive.

A few days after having this prophetic dream, I was amazed to find that a well-known peace organization, **Hamnesty International**, had indeed sent Porky Pig on a Mideast peace mission. Although the Israelis have temporarily detained the plucky porker at the border ("Something about this whole thing just doesn't seem kosher," said one official), I predict that Porky's bravery will bring all fighting to an end, as he plants himself between warring factions on the West Bank, waves his pig's knuckles in the air, and says, "Th-Th-Th-That's All, Folks!"

• • •

Dear Swami:

I recently read a disturbing account of repression in the Baltic countries. A pro-democracy demonstration in Estonia was broken up by military police. Demonstrators were shoved, and a few were even thrown to the pavement and injured. With all the talk about moving towards democracy in Eastern Europe and the former Soviet Republics, don't you think this is awfully hypocritical?

Cy Beria,
Shamokin, Pennsylvania

Dear Cy:

It certainly is. People who live in glasnost houses shouldn't throw Estonians.

• • •

97

Dear Swami:

Do you follow politics? If so, what is your take on Ross Perot? Is he a civic-minded supercitizen, or just a paranoid megalomaniac?

Billy Yuss,
Roanoake, Virginia

Dear Billy:

I tried following politics for awhile, but I just kept going around in circles. That's when I realized that politics had no idea where it was going, so it was kind of senseless to follow it. Maybe if we started leading politics instead, we'd all be better off. That's where your friend Ross Perot comes in. He volunteered to lead politics toward a change, which is admirable. However, for someone whose pitch is fiscal fitness, Mr. Perot doesn't seem all that prudent to me. I mean, he told us he was willing to spend $100 million for the office of President. A President only gets paid $200,000 a year. He'd have to hold office 500 years just to break even. What's so smart about that? If he's going to spend that kind of money on a public office, it should at least come with a President already in it!

A better idea would be to buy Congress. That seems to be where the real problem is anyway. For 435 Representatives and 100 Senators, the $100 million would break down to about $186,915.89 per member. Who knows? A bonus like that might actually counterbalance the contributions they are receiving from the oil and lumber industries and other special interest groups, and it might even nudge them to vote in the public interest. I kept hoping that Perot would buy air time last July 4th to announce to the American people, "Say folks, I just bought a birthday present for yuh—Congress!" But alas, it never happened.

As for the Perot candidacy, I think it was a big letdown, what with his dropping out to avoid close scrutiny and then re-entering at the last minute. Instead of being the big cheese everybody thought he was, Ross Perot turned out to be "Ross Perogi"—a little cheese surrounded by a whole lotta dough.

• • •

Dear Swami:

I was very disturbed by the Rodney King verdict and the resulting riots in Los Angeles. Are we ever going to solve the problem of racism in this society?

Enya Face,
Chicago, Illinois

Dear Enya:

*In order to solve the problem of racism, we must first deal with the problem of **Erase-ism.** That's where all parties involved try to erase their own responsibility for the mess we're in. For the past twelve years or so, white society has practiced erase-ism by pretending there's no racial karma in this country. To hear white erase-ists talk, African-Americans just showed up on our shores one day looking for a government hand-out and an NBA contract. Slavery? It's been repressed, and I'll tell you why. Because we owe African-Americans. And you know how it is when you owe somebody—you don't want to see them. It's so-called human nature to actively avoid what makes us uncomfortable, and nothing makes us as uncomfortable as guilt. And in spite of all protestations that "my* great-grandfather didn't have slaves," all white people feel this guilt. They look at an African-American and see someone whose enslaved ancestors never collected their last paycheck, let alone their first. And as a result, white people cannot look them in the "I."

And so in order for both races to see "I-to-I," there must be an unconditional apology, and the apology must be unconditionally accepted. How about a Guinness Book World Record Greeting Card, maybe 50 feet high, that is signed by all white Americans regardless of whether their ancestors had slaves or not? It'd certainly make us white folks feel good to finally go to confession after all these years. And who doesn't like receiving a greeting card in the mail, especially if it's 50 feet high and has forty or fifty million signatures on it? Now of course, it wouldn't be too far out of line for the recipients of this huge apology card to shake it to see if some money falls out.

Now Erase-ism exists in the African-American community as well. Erase-ists there are denying any responsibility for the conditions in their own community and are childishly waiting for someone to fix it for them. I got news for you. If you want repairmen to come to your neighborhood, you'd better welcome them with open arms (and I don't mean firearms, either). You want food and other goods, protection from crime, people to teach your children, and when these people come into your community you shoot at them? Then you burn down your own neighborhood, but not before looting all the stores. Hey, that's where I want to invest **MY** money! Wake up, people. You must stop condoning the shortsighted actions of a few hoodlums and start standing up for decency. Don't be afraid to look outside your community for friends and allies. Like the Koreans. Don't trash them because they're successful, learn from them. After all, they've paid some dues, so why not accept them as the Seoul Brothers they are?

• • •

Dear Swami:

I have heard stories that former Soviet leader Gorbachev has been offered a visiting professorship at several American universities. Can you predict whether he will accept any of these positions?

Alison Wanda Land,
Ithaca, New York

Dear Alison:

Actually, I think he will end up turning them down for financial reasons. After all, the universities couldn't possibly compete with salaries paid in the private sector, unless of course Gorbachev were to be signed as a football coach. And given the fact that the last team he coached led the world in fumbles, lost about a trillion yards in its last season, and isn't even in the league anymore, that's sort of doubtful. No, my usually reliable sources tell me that Gorby is headed for Tinseltown to star in a new situation comedy about a lovable yet bumbling Russian submarine commander who spends most of his time trying to scrounge supplies for his ill-equipped boat and mediating between arguing crew members. So watch for "Mikhail's Navy" to make its debut next fall.

• • •

Dear Swami:

Just last year, all you heard at the Republican convention was family values, family values, family values. Now it comes out that George Bush's three sons all were involved in questionable dealings and received special treatment from the government. Now I ask you, Swami, what kind of family values are these?

Morely Upright,
Spartansburg, South Carolina

101

Dear Morely:

The Gambino Family?

• • •

Dear Swami:

I notice that we're ready to send money to help stave off starvation in the Soviet republics but are not willing to help the homeless in our own cities. Who is to blame for this situation?

Pancho Leitzaut,
Miami, Florida

Dear Pancho:

I'm afraid the homeless themselves must bear the responsibility, because it was they who made a serious tactical error. If only they had built nuclear weapons instead of cardboard shelters, they'd be getting a lot more respect.

• • •

Dear Swami:

I recently read in one of those supermarket tabloids that Lee Harvey Oswald was actually an alien from a planet very similar to Krypton in the Superman story. He was possessed of remarkable powers which allowed him to fly at warp speed and just about be in two places at once so that he could easily fire bullets from two different locations. The Kennedy assassination was part of an intergalactic plot to stop the spread of "surfing music"—which in fact mysteriously abated shortly after the fateful day in Dallas. What do you think?

Lona Sassin,
Columbus, Ohio

Dear Lona:

It's a bit far-fetched, but it certainly makes more sense than the Warren Commission Report. I mean, even the name "Warren Commission" suggests questionable reliability. Had it been called the Lion's Den Commission, that would be pretty authoritative. But naming a commission after a hutch of rabbits, I don't know. All I can see are these timid committee members, noses twitching, afraid to really get to the truth. As for the truth, as usual your supermarket tabloid is only half right. The part about Oswald being an alien is correct. But as far as the motive goes, they've totally missed the boat. The question any good investigator would ask is, who would benefit if Mr. Kennedy were out of the picture? And the answer is so simple that it almost escapes notice. In what way was President Kennedy different from every president since the days of Lincoln? I'll tell you the answer. He didn't wear a hat. In fact, he refused to wear a hat. And in emulation of the President's style, millions of men stopped wearing hats as well. As for the multinational hatmakers, well they were as mad as hatters. My theory is that the late President was done in by the millinery industrial complex.

• • •

Dear Swami:

I've been reading about the folks who have been busted for baking marijuana brownies for AIDS patients, and I think it's totally ridiculous. Surely, there are more important things for us to spend our valuable human and financial resources on—cleaning up the environment, for example. What do you think, Swami? How do we go about having marijuana legalized? By the way, I understand marijuana is legal in Alaska. Do you know anything about that?

Bliss Stout,
Hempstead, New York

Dear Bliss:

Yes, it is true that possession of marijuana has been legal in Alaska, and the reason is quite simple. As you know, parts of Alaska are very close to the Arctic Circle, and as such they may go two or three months without seeing the sun. This makes pursuing court cases very difficult. I mean, can you imagine an attorney asking the defendant, "Where were you on the night of November 30th to February 15th?"

As for legalization elsewhere, I agree with you that weed killer is far more dangerous in the long run than killer weed, but I think you've got a hard row to hoe, so to speak. Among our younger generation, marijuana's popularity has been superseded by an even more powerful mood-altering substance—money. Not only that, but people in general have become more health-conscious, and the smoking of anything (including herring, for that matter) has fallen out of favor. This anti-smoking sentiment has gotten so strong, incidentally, that many smokers have taken to attending Native American ceremonies just so they can have a guiltless hit of tobacco. But I predict that this very health-consciousness will provide the open door for legalization. All you have to do is publicize a newly-discovered disease called MDS—Marijuana Deprivation Syndrome. Symptoms include: obsession with status and financial achievement, inability to be in the present moment, and chronic seriousness which can become laugh-threatening. Miraculously, just a small weekly dose of marijuana can offset these symptoms and restore homeostasis (that's where you stay home and listen to your old Firesign Theater albums and eat Screaming Yellow Zonkers). I'm sure that as soon as the medical journals get hold of this information, it won't be too long before you'll be able to get prescriptions for cannibis just like any other drug.

Meanwhile, there is another, more important development. As you probably know, the brain itself produces the very chemicals that get us high. Unbeknownst to the Drug Enforcement Administration, subversive hypnotherapists across the country are actually teaching former drug-gies to produce the very high they used to pay for by releasing these chemicals in their own brains! Not only do these leave no trace of any offending drug in the bloodstream, but there are none of the "coming down" symptoms of real drugs. Sure, the day will come when many jobs will have mandatory brain chemistry testing to uncover any loose brain-stems, or the DEA will fly helicopters over fields looking for clusters of smiling faces, but until that happens I suggest you forget the high you can buy out on the streets—and grow your own inside your head.

• • •

Dear Swami:

I just finished watching my videotape of the 1993 Inauguration festivities and it's a little bit scary to think of the rock 'n' roll generation in the White House. What do you make of Al Gore's dancing, anyway?

Stan Dupp,
Pottstown, Pennsylvania

Dear Stan:

I'm kind of at a loss on this one. I didn't understand Al Gore Rhythms back in college, and I guess I still don't. Why don't you ask Dr. Science instead?

• • •

Dear Swami:

Tell me, please. Will there be true arms control before the end of the century?

Klaus Trafobik,
Berlin, Germany

Dear Klaus:

Unfortunately, the prevailing belief that good defenses make good neighbors will make this virtually impossible. However, there is some good news. Despite lack of progress on arms control, underarms control will be a reality before the year 2000. With the help of Proctor & Gamble and several other deodorant makers, a worldwide Underarms Control Treaty will be reached by 1998. Sadly, wars will still take place but when troops mount offensive positions, they'll be a little less offensive. As a great contemporary philosopher once said, "Our water is unsafe, our air is unsafe, our soil is unsafe, our streets are unsafe. But under our arms—we're completely safe."

• • •

Dear Swami:

I'm concerned about the sharp increase in the crime rate in this country. The latest statistics show that crime is up 15% over last year. Tell me Swami, will the growing new age awareness reverse this trend?

> Anais Lass,
> Bronx, New York

Dear Anais:

I would not place too much hope on the coming of some enlightened new age. In fact, new age meccas such as Boulder, Sedona and Santa Cruz have actually developed their own kinds of crime. In Sedona, for example, there has been an epidemic of new age white collar crime—people falsifying their astrological charts for job applications. And Santa Cruz recently has seen roving gangs of restless youths invading psychic space and defacing auras. Perhaps the most serious problem has been in Boulder, which has been overrun by new age muggers. When they take your money, they ask, "Why did you create this?" And when they leave, they say, "Thank you for sharing."

• • •

Dear Swami:

How do you explain the suffering of all those on the planet who do not have enough to eat?

Gil Tridden,
Scarsdale, New York

Dear Gil:

That is easy to explain. What is harder to explain is the suffering of all those on the planet who have too much to eat.

• • •

Dear Swami:

This entire Mideast situation has me extremely upset. We sent our troops over there to die for the Kuwaitis and Saudis who treat their women like little more than chattel. Even as we approach the 21st Century, women in these Arab countries must dutifully walk ten feet behind their husbands. I saw very little about this in the press. What's your opinion, Swami?

Fern Natchoor
Berkeley, California

Dear Fern:

I, too, find this archaic attitude towards women deplorable. After dong a bit of research, I have discovered that the war has actually changed some of these traditional customs, if not the underlying values. Western reporters in these countries say that women are now encouraged to walk ahead of their husbands. This is expected to continue at least until all the hidden land mines are discovered.

• • •

Dear Swami:

I am deeply concerned that the Ku Klux Klan seems to be marching again. Sure, they are small in numbers, but just their presence gives me the creeps. Can anything be done to demonstrate that the Klan attitude must not be taken into the next century? Isn't it about time we stopped discriminating against people just because of pigmentation?

Sybil Reitz,
Baltimore, Maryland

Dear Sybil:

I feel the same way you do about those sheet-heads, but we must not get sucked into hating them. Instead, we must surround them with so much love that there is no room for them to escape into hatred. Imagine a Klan rally being surrounded by thousands of people joining hands in a very large circle lovingly singing, "We Love You Sheet-heads, Oh Yes We Do" drowning out all their hate slogans. For just as the white cells in the human body surround cancer cells, we must contain the malignancy of hatred by surrounding it with healing energy. In that sense, every Klan rally is an opportunity for the body politic to strengthen its immune system. We must not repress the Klan. Give them the right to speech and assembly so that their hatred can be brought to light, discussed, and neutralized. Yes, pigmentation is a very poor way to determine rights in a society. Well, we can't stop the pigs from mentating, but we can make sure they don't feed on our fears and prejudices.

• • •

Dear Swami:

What about the terrible situation in the former Yugoslavia? Is there anything we can do to help bring lasting peace to the Balkans?

> Olive Branch,
> Asheville, North Carolina

Dear Olive:

It's not an easy situation. They didn't name the place the "Balkans" for nothing. These people have been Balkan at cooperating for centuries. Given the atrocities that have been perpetrated down through history by all sides, it would be easy for us just to say, "Serbs 'em right" and sit back and watch "Mission Impossible" re-runs. But what about those people over there who are ready to heal their hearts and go on a low-assault regimen? We can't just abandon them. We can't get our way by bombing them. And we can't just leave them alone. This is truly a dilemma.

But as my guru Harry Cohen Baba once told me, when you're faced with a dilemma, the only thing to do is make dilemmanade. Yes, we need a new approach, something truly revolutionary and earth-shaking. Here's what I suggest: Get yourself one of those soft "Hug-a-planets" or even a traditional globe. Find the former Yugoslavia on the globe. Then, gently touch and softly massage the sore spot on the planet. Pretend it is a child who has just skinned his knee. Say soothing words. Kiss the boo-boo. Don't laugh. This may work. Here's why:

1. You ever see those voodoo guys sticking pins in a doll? If it didn't work, would they do it? If a curse works, surely a blessing will work at least as well, right?

2. There could be a whole new way to watch the news. An entire family watching CNN, each with a Hug-a-planet in their lap, massaging all the trouble spots until the tension disperses.

3. The Serbs are particularly macho. The thought of millions of people cooing and slobbering over their country might drive them to the negotiating table out of sheer disgust.

4. I recently spoke with Ross Perot, and he wholeheartedly endorses the plan: "Now this is a foreign policy I can go for. It costs next to nothing. It gets families doing things together just like in the old days. And if we play our cards right, we can regenerate our economy by manufacturing cuddly little stuffed planets."

5. Imagine churches, synagogues, mosques and temples all over the country dispensing with the usual stuff and instead everyone sitting and stroking these little Earths and saying loving words. Of course, there are bound to be some protests about meddlesome Americans praying on some unsuspecting nation. Nevertheless, a usually reliable source says that God is enthusiastic about the idea. "Frankly," the Eternal One says, "I've gotten out of the habit of attending religious services, except for those fun gospel churches where everyone sings and claps and gets sweaty. But who knows? If this sort of thing happens, I might start going again."

• • •

Dear Swami:

Why is it that for centuries and centuries spiritual masters have been speaking out against war, and yet generation after generation we continue to have more frequent—and more horrible—wars? I am serious about this, Swami, and I want a serious answer.

Israel Bummer,
Skokie, Illinois

Dear Israel:

*You want a serious answer, and a serious answer you will get. I want you to think about exactly what spiritual leaders have been telling people for centuries. They have been saying, "Treat everyone like your brother and sister." And that of course is the source of the problem. Can you remember how you treated your brothers or sisters? And how they treated you? You pulled each other's hair, pinched, slapped, slugged, sadistically tickled, and otherwise tortured one another. And then, one or both of you would go running to Mommy or Daddy saying, "S(he) started it!" A perfect model for the world we have today—sibling rivalry between the world's religions and cultures with everyone pointing fingers and saying "Look what **he** did!" and doing all they can to prove themselves superior in their Father's eye.*

If we want people to disarm, we must use a disarming metaphor. That's why I recommend that we forget this damaging brother and sister stuff and instead treat other people as if they were puppies—pet them, feed them, play with them, and bathe in the unconditional love that comes in return. Think of it. If we all begin to see each other as innocent, loving puppies, we'll finally realize that there's no "we" vs. "they," just "us." And we all know there can never be lasting peace until there's just-us in the world.

*Remember back between the World Wars when France developed an "impenetrable" defense called the Maginot Line? What we need now is an Imaginot Line. Imagine no line between countries. Imagine a time when those who insist on borderlines will be termed "borderline personalities" and ignored. Now **that's** an impenetrable defense.*

• • •

Dear Swami:

Now that the 1992 election is over, how will history treat Dan Quayle?

Ray-Pierre Witt,
Montreal, Quebec

Dear Ray:

Dan Quayle will have a very definite place in history. He will be remembered as the only politician in history to pick a fight with a fictional character—and lose.

Environmentalism: The <u>Real</u> "Right to Life" Movement

Remember the Alaskan oil spill and how we felt when we saw pictures of dying birds covered with sludge? It's true the oily bird gets the attention—but by then it's too late. We are all used to waiting until we have a disaster and then taking emergency measures. Maybe it's time we took Emerge 'N' See measures instead. That is where we emerge from our short-sighted dependency on nonrenewable fuels and see how we can work within the delicate balance of nature. I know this sounds awfully serious, but I'm not the only one who feels this way. Mother Earth is rapidly losing her sense of humus, and when this Mother has a toxic reaction, look out. You or I might break out in acne. She breaks out in volcanoes!

Yes, it is a jungle out there. And it's a good thing. Because trees and plants are our planet's respiratory system. So it's time to turn over a new leaf. All this money spent trying to reach out to other planets, how about reaching out to our own? Let's not worry about the little green guys from outer space and let's focus instead on the little green guys in our own backyard—because they are rooting for us. Let us never forget the valuable gift the Creator gave us on the Third Day when He said, "This Bud's for you."

Now please understand that the Swami is not trying to change the world. Because there's an easier way. If we can just toilet-train the world, we'll never need to change it again.

• • •

Dear Swami:

The huge oil spill in Alaska was a great tragedy, but in our rush to blame Exxon, I think we overlooked the real problem—substance abuse. After all, wasn't the captain under the influence of alcohol and thus unable to do his job? When are we going to stop blaming corporations and other institutions for our personal weaknesses and face up to the problem that threatens our very social fiber—chemical dependency?

Jim Nastik,
Akron, Ohio

Dear Jim:

You're absolutely right. I think chemical dependency is the greatest social problem facing the world today. We have become much too dependent on chemicals in all aspects of our lives. And these chemicals can cause dangerous delusions, particularly the delusion that we need them to fuel our vehicles, grow our food, and medicate our bodies. Petrochemical pushers have gotten the soil so addicted to herbicides and pesticides that it cannot produce without them. These substances have turned a once proud and vital land into a sniveling weakling waiting for its next injection of Rapid-Gro. That is why I am launching my worldwide campaign to **JUST SAY NO TO CHEMICAL DEPENDENCY.**

We are abusing substances like crazy—substances like our air, our water, our life-giving soil. This is the kind of substance abuse that really damages unborn fetuses, not to mention born ones. Scientists say the poisons in our soil, our atmosphere and our water will be affecting the heir quality for many years to come. So if you're truly interested in "right to life" issues, I suggest helping our planet kick the chemical habit and go organic. Let's check the planet into a good detox program and get our soil high on life, otherwise there will be no life to get high on. And let's restore the rain forests as the first step in a planetary aerobics program to make sure our Mother Earth stays fit for life.

• • •

Dear Swami:

I've been working in the chemical industry for nearly ten years now. My wife and I have been trying to start a family, but with no success. I recently read a report that certain chemicals can cause sterility, however I've been assured by my company that this is not true. Do you know anything about this?

Gene Poole,
Midland, Texas

Dear Gene:

Well, since the industry denies any connection between chemical exposure and your situation, the only possible conclusion is that sterility is inherited. And this makes sense. If your parents were sterile it stands to reason that you should be too.

• • •

Dear Swami:

I don't know what all the fuss is about the environment. Don't people know that the pollution and environmental destruction have been predicted in the Bible? Personally, I see it as a positive thing because it means we are fast approaching the day of the Lord's Reign on Earth. When the King returns (and I'm not talking about Elvis here), all that is wrong will be made right, all that is unclean will be made pure, and the righteous will dwell in God's

Mansion. So stop fussing about a few dead fish. Turn your back on the mess, and turn your face to the Light.

> Reggie Mentid,
> Oklahoma City, Oklahoma

Dear Reggie:

I too have read the predictions that the Lord will be returning soon, and as far as I'm concerned that's all the more reason to clean up the environment. After all, if you just got a letter that your Aunt Matilda was coming from Omaha to visit, you'd certainly straighten your place up a bit—and you're not even that crazy about Aunt Matilda. Doesn't Jesus rate a similar treatment? We've been inviting this Guy for two millenia now, and all we're going to say to Him when He arrives is, "Great to see you. By the way, we left this mess for you. Would you mind cleaning it up?" I don't think so. Sure, He's a compassionate fellow and all that, but I have it on good authority that He's spent the last thousand years or so working on His co-dependency issues—so don't expect Him to dispose of your garbage in exchange for your worshipping Him. Believe me, He's had it with dysfunctional relationships (especially in the light of how He got nailed the last time).

No, this time He's not getting involved until He sees how we are in our other relationships—with other living things on the planet as well as our fellow human beings. Sure, He will forgive anyone and everyone. But no way is He going to be an enabler for a planet-batterer. My guru Harry Cohen Baba put it more bluntly: "You want to dwell in the Mansion of the Lord? At the very least, you gotta be housebroken."

• • •

Dear Swami:

A while back, I heard about that terrible derailment and chemical spill up there near Mt. Shasta, California—and then all of a sudden, we just stopped hearing anything about it. I did see a little blurb in *the Wall Street Journal*, though, that said that a few fish had died but basically the problem was under control. Do you have any further news on the situation?

Lowen N. Seid,
Cleveland Heights, Ohio

Dear Lowen:

There's a very good reason why you haven't heard much about the spill, and that's because the chemical companies are using the latest new age approaches for handling the problem. That's right. In an official communication to the community of Mt. Shasta, company officials said: **"This chemical spill is an illusion, so we have decided the best way to handle the situation is by not giving it any energy. Because as you know, what you think about expands, and we wouldn't want to create any more experiences like this, would we? Sure your tourist business is ruined, but try to see the perfection in this. As for the fish and animals who have had to make their transition, this is just part of their lesson this time around.**

"Meanwhile, we are working hard to rectify the situation. First of all, we are recommending a full-scale investigation into why you people attracted this situation into your lives. Secondly, we very much believe that negativity is the root cause of problems like these, so we are discouraging any negative mention of the spill. That is why we have instructed news media people to downplay the story, or else they will surely attract negative karma into their lives—possibly in this lifetime, even.

"So as you do your meditation this evening, you can relax in the knowledge that our Disaster Containment Team is doing everything possible to prevent a misfortune from turning into a disaster. The spill is surely a misfortune. Being held accountable for it, now _that_ would be a disaster."

• • •

Dear Swami:

I am very concerned with the growing hole in the ozone layer due to environmental pollutants. Is there anything from the Swami's point of view that can be done about this?

Dewey Matter,
Red Bank, New Jersey

Dear Dewey:

Actually, the real problem is with the Bozone Layer. The Bozone Layer is a thickening of the skull which causes the delusion that the ozone layer is of little importance and it is okay to keep destroying it. Personally, I am very concerned with our planet's bald spot. The Earth is much too young to be losing its ozone. Fortunately, there is something that can be done. As you probably know, the use of styrofoam for packing material and fast-food cups and containers is contributing to the ozone problem. So I suggest that we replace styrofoam with something that has basically the same consistency, but is slightly more biodegradable—rice cakes.

• • •

Dear Swami:

As a native of Oregon, I have watched the battles between environmentalists and logging companies with growing sadness and frustration. Don't the logging companies realize that when they clear-cut old growth forests, they are destroying an irreplaceable resource? If only they could see the wisdom in saving the old trees. Tell me, Swami, is there even the slightest glimmer of hope?

Joaquin DeWoods,
Dexter, Oregon

Dear Joaquin:

Of course there is. In response to the criticism that they don't care about saving ancient trees, several major logging companies have hired scores of revivalist preachers and sent them into old growth forests to do just that. That way, when the trees are cut down they will be assured of going to heaven. Unfortunately, losing these trees is hell for the rest of us.

• • •

Dear Swami:

I've recently become attracted to veganism—that is where you consume no animal products—and it rather seems like a good idea to me, truly the wave of the future. What do you think, Swami?

Colin Clense,
Brighton, England

Dear Colin,

I, too, have heard predictions that in the future backyard barbecues will be used only to teach toddlers firewalking. Nevertheless, all I can think about when I think of veganism is hundreds and thousands of cows, unhappy and confused, standing in the unemployment lines. Because it would be cruel indeed to turn these domestic animals out into the woods to fend for themselves—hey, there're hardly woods left for animals who **like** living in the woods. So we would have to subsidize these creatures, and we don't even like subsidizing poor people. And how would these cattle feel being put out to pasture in the prime of their productive years?

Unemployed chickens would present an even greater problem. If we stopped eating their eggs, these eggs would hatch into—more chickens! In this vegan future you talk about I can just see homeless chickens living on the street like pigeons and squirrels, only not nearly as endear-

ing—especially those noisy roosters. And when hordes of chickens march on Washington looking for jobs—I tell you, if you think there's some chickenshit in Washington now, wait until the chickens really come home to roost. Oh, I foresee terrible difficulties—abortion clinics for chickens, drugs to induce henopause...

Now I am the first to insist that working conditions for these creatures must improve, because our cruel and disrespectful treatment of animals will have grave karmic implications. But we must remember that animals have karma to burn off too, and their karma yoga is to give to us kindly. (Is it not interesting that we never hear the phrase, "the soy protein of human kindness?") So let's give animals their rights in the workplace and accept their willingness to give. Even if we do not ask our cattle to give hamburger, still we can ask them for milk. Surely there's no beef with that.

• • •

Dear Swami:

Do you believe there are extraterrestrials among us? I saw this movie where extraterrestrials were all over the place and looked just like ordinary people. And they would get married to humans, and their children would be extraterrestrials as well. This movie seemed very real to me, and I began to wonder—are extraterrestrials taking over the planet? And if so, do they pose a threat? In other words, Swami, do you see any space wars in our future?

Helena Handbasket,
Brattleboro, Vermont

Dear Helena:

I'm glad you asked that question. It is my belief that extra terrestrials represent the single greatest threat to our planet, and I have the statistics to prove it. Compared to thirty years ago, we have three billion extra terrestrials. That's already more terrestrials than we've ever had on this planet, and we're approaching our limits. That movie you mentioned is all too real, because it is indeed ordinary people who are bringing these extra terrestrials into the world.

And I have news for you. Those space wars are already happening, thanks to these extra terrestrials. Because for every extra terrestrial, there needs to be extra territory. Never mind the Challenger and the Discovery—the real race for space is happening right here on Earth, and that is why there is so much fighting today. It's purely a matter of arithmetic—as long as we humans keep multiplying, we're going to stay divided.

And of course to house and feed all these extra terrestrials, we have had to destroy much of the natural environment, particularly the forests. That is why I am very much in favor of this new worldwide organization which advocates raising trees instead of children—it's called Plant Parenthood. Yes, it's time to launch a new Space Program, one which shifts the focus from the race for outer space to our own planet—otherwise, our whole race will be outta space.

• • •

Dear Swami:

I notice a lot of show business people and rock stars are doing benefits for the environment. I'm a big country music fan, and I'm wondering if you know of an environmental music event featuring country music.

Linda Hand,
Louisville, Kentucky

Dear Linda:

I sure do. It seems that a whole legion of stars from Nashville are putting on a show this summer to preserve the habitats of waterfowl, and it's called Grand Ole Osprey. And they have a compelling slogan that I know will catch on: "More waterfowl, less foul water."

• • •

Dear Swami:

I wonder how many energy crises and Gulf Wars are going to be needed before we Americans—not to mention the other industrialized nations—develop a sane energy-use policy. Swami, do you have any insights as to how we can shift the focus away from nuclear and fossil fuels, and use more renewable resources?

Cora N. Janeers,
Boulder, Colorado

Dear Cora:

I'm with you. Talk about deficit spending! The Earth has been painstakingly saving up fossil fuels for millions of years, and we go on a spending binge and blow the whole wad in a couple of decades. If our grandchildren ever do a movie about our generation, it'll probably be called Honey, I Shrunk the Inheritance. And if old "penny-saved, penny-earned" Ben Franklin came back today, he'd probably turn us all over his knee and thrash us with a gasoline pump hose.

That's the bad news. But every acid rain cloud has a silver lining (or is that mercury?) and this is no exception. I believe we can solve the energy mess and become stronger and healthier by combining physical fitness with fiscal fitness. Now, how many of you reading this go to health clubs? You drive to your health club, and then spend an hour or so biking on a stationary bike, running on a treadmill, climbing imaginary stairs, or pumping iron. Then, the building has to be air conditioned to cool you down! What a waste of energy.

I propose we build a combination health club/power station in every community. All the bikes, stairsteps, treadmills and weight machines will be hooked up to a generator. And folks will be encouraged to convert the calories they're burning off into energy for their community. Talk about making a contribution and giving of yourself! Do you realize how many pounds are shed (and regained) in this country each year? Why not have your loss be everybody's gain?

As for downtown traffic, I recommend we bring back rickshas. What about all those young athletes who spend their days in training, not to mention those who enjoy running, jogging, and power walking for no good reason? Why not have two or three or four of them get together and pull a ricksha for a few hours? It can be called "Burn While You Earn," and can help offset the cost of athletic scholarships. And pulling together this way will help develop teamwork, at least as well as a war does. Maybe by using the most renewable resources we have, our own human power, we can begin to pay back our Mother for giving us an advance on our allowance.

• • •

Dear Swami:

Don't you think this environmental thing has gotten out of hand? The whole idea of global warming is nothing but a scam, and we're sacrificing our entire economic system and hard-won prosperity to save some pathetic snail darter or some such thing who'd become extinct in a couple of million years anyway. And those _Earth First!_ terrorists? Don't tell me the Cold War is over. I know where the Communists have gone—they've become "environmentalists." Watermelons, I call them—green on the outside, red on the inside. What's your opinion of these arrogant so-called "defenders of the Earth?"

Upton O. Goode,
Grosse Point, Michigan

Dear Upton:

I must agree that there is something very patronizing about "defending the Earth," as if the Earth can't take care of itself. Try being in the middle of a hurricane, tornado, earthquake or volcano and see who needs defending. But I think this endangered species thing is worth looking into. Most environmentalists are concerned with saving one endangered species in particular, namely the human species. Or as my own guru Harry Cohen Baba used to say, "The Earth will indeed be restored to a pristine state—I certainly hope we humans are around to enjoy it."

Environmentalists are even more clever than you think. They're clever enough to know that it's not the Earth which may not survive the onslaught of human endeavor, but us. They know that as "civilization" feasts on the fruits of industry, millions of humans are slowly dying from domain poisoning. That is where the domains of fresh air, clean water and healthy soil have all been poisoned by carelessly prepared goods. The fact that domain poisoning doesn't necessarily kill right away makes it even more insidious. Long before actual death comes unconsciousness, a stage which many believe we have already entered. Witness our election of Reagan and Bush for twelve years.

Groups such as Earth First! are providing the shock therapy to rouse the body politic from its chemical-induced stupor. Now let's face it, no one likes shock therapy, especially when they're in a deep sleep and having this wonderful dream that it's the '50s again. I see these "extremist" groups as Minutemen who are shouting an early warning that our freedom to eat, drink and breathe is being threatened by a latter-day colonial power that has taxed our planetary resources for short-term financial gain. Environmentalists are true planetary patriots and I support them in their "Our planet—love it or leave it!" attitude. Let us hope they are able to strike terra into the hearts of men so that we base our economic prosperity on what we can create in harmony with the planet rather than what we can steal from future generations.

As for the folks who deny that we have an environmental problem so that they can make their short-term profits, the Swami has a name for them. Gourds, I call them—hard on the outside, empty on the inside.

• • •

Dear Swami:

Here I am trying to teach my family environmental awareness, and my husband is driving me crazy. While I am very environmentally correct, he has about zero environmental consciousness. He thinks "recycling" means using the same bike path over and over again, he uses weed killers on our lawn, and he insists on driving a luxury car instead of the Hondas that everyone else around here has. Frankly, I'm embarrassed by him and I'm even considering divorce. Any advice?

Burdonna Wyer,
Concord, California

Dear Burdonna:

I can certainly sympathize with your plight. Environmental awareness is a good thing but I have noticed a disturbing phenomenon in many communities—greenness envy. That is where there is much unhealthy competition to see who is more environmentally aware. And this has led to unnecessary self-sacrifice. Sure, it is fine to be a tree-hugger, but if you insist on hugging cactus you deserve all the needling you get. So lighten up. By all means keep trying to educate your husband. If he insists on using herbicides, tell him Swami's official definition: Weed killers are chemical substances that kill living things, some of which are weeds.

125

As for the kind of car he drives, auto-suggestion might be helpful. Each night before as he is dozing off, quietly whisper in his ear, "Driving a Honda is good carma, driving a Honda is good carma." But even if you don't reach an Accord with your husband, don't despair. Some great enlightened beings still drive luxury cars, as my Japanese counterpart Swami Beyondahonda can testify. And please think twice before tossing your marriage by the side of the road. Throwaway bottles can muck up the landscape, but all indications are that throwaway relationships can do even worse.

• • •

Dear Swami:

You know, it's interesting to me to see spiritual folks talk about how Mother Earth is so sweet and gentle, and how She is endangered by big, bad humans with their evil technology. And then in the course of one short month, we see the devastation wrought by Hurricane Hugo and the earthquake in the Bay Area. Ironically, it is technology in the form of the latest building techniques which prevented more death and destruction during the quake. How about it, Swami. Does Mother Earth have it in for us, or is She just not as perfect as once believed?

Maj. Gen. Newcombe Gladley,
Rocky Flats, Colorado

Dear General:

Certainly technology is beneficial. I for one am very grateful that I can now reach many more people traveling by plane than I did a couple of lifetimes ago when I had to travel by mule. So I applaud technology for getting us off our asses and into a more accelerated growth pattern. But there is a downside. We humans have become obsessed with the man-made. We forget we are immortal in Spirit, so we try to build physical structures that last forever. And this unresolved Edifice Complex has been the cause of much human suffering. So Mother Earth has taken it upon Herself to show us that we must build our lives on a firmer foundation. And She will create peace on Earth, even if She personally has to turn us all into Quakers to do it.

The truth is Mother Earth loves us dearly, but just as the most loving human mother is not perfect, so She has her faults as well. But when we are aware of these faults and we build on them anyway, whose fault is it? So my advice for avoiding earth-shattering consequences is simple: When you find a fault, don't dwell on it.

• • •

Dear Swami:

I know a lot of work has been done with animal consciousness and communicating with this particular life form. What about vegetables? What do they want in life? Do they resent us eating them, or what? Please tell us, Swami.

Lucinda Woods,
Redding, California

Dear Lucinda:

You came to the right Swami with this question. During my apprenticeship with the Native American shaman Broken Wind, I learned the moss code which enabled me to converse with the plant kingdom. I can tell you right off the bat that it is just fine with vegetables that we eat them. For that is their purpose. Sure beets feel uprooted when they are picked and carrots sometimes have nightmares about juicer blades. But they know that in order to progress, reincarnationally speaking, they must be truly useful. (In that sense, they are more advanced than many humans.) Even animals are aware of the rewards for this kind of service. Why do you think chickens keep reincarnating? For the frequent-fryer bonus points, of course!

Getting back to vegetables, they are a lot like us, for they certainly have their opinions. Fruits and vegetables don't like to mix much, but they both absolutely abhor weed killers—competition builds character, they believe. And they feel the same way about pesticides. A militant young Spartan apple I spoke with recently was very adamant about this issue: "We are all forced to compete at an early age with that Hollywood image of an apple, the Red Delicious. Delicious? Give me a break! She's just swathed with tons of cosmetic pesticides to make sure she's got no unsightly blemishes. But her beauty's only skin deep. If she had any taste, she wouldn't need all that make-up. Fortunately, I think the natural look is coming back."

All in all, I think we can learn something from the way fruits and vegetables approach life. We often forget where we fit in the old food cycle. I mean, we think we invented the food processor when actually plants had them first. Earthworms, they are called. Yes, I think we'll all be a lot better off when we see things in perspective and realize that everybody's somebody's fuel and we're all gonna end up as worm patoots someday.

• • •

Dear Swami:

There's a huge controversy in our local school system whether or not to teach about birth control. Although it is obvious that young people are engaging in unprotected sex, many influential local church leaders are insisting that the only form of birth control that should be talked about in school is abstinence. Meanwhile, other groups are talking about actually handing out condoms in school. What do you think, Swami?

Bea Fareel,
Vista, California

Dear Bea:

I wish these religious leaders would get with the program. I mean, as long as population control is based on copulation control it will never work. You can never buck the biological imperative. Or as one of those televangelists caught with his pants down remarked, "If God didn't mean for us guys to follow our little thing around, he wouldn't have put it in front." And what about all the controversy about priests molesting little children? My goodness, if there are **priests** who can't stay celibate, what about those folks who aren't even trying? Instead of offering a condemnation of sexuality, religious leaders would do better to support a condom nation instead. Could we do worse if we gave our young people condoms to play with instead of guns? We'd have fewer children having children, fewer children killing children—and those still bent on violence could have terrific water balloon fights.

• • •

Dear Swami:

I am very concerned about the problems of overpopulation. It is obvious that the planet cannot support many more of us. I am worried, aren't you?

Moe Mentiss,
Boise, Idaho

Dear Moe:

Nah, I'm not worried at all. I used to be, until I began to think about it logically. I realized that despite all the great breakthroughs in theoretical science, most folks on the planet are still back in the days of Descartes. Which is good news. Because as you know Descartes said, "I think, therefore I am." The better news is, people are thinking less and less all the time! So it is simple. By building more malls, giving our kids more video games, and putting them in front of the TV for hours and hours—not to mention the discouragement of actual thinking they usually get in school—we will successfully eliminate thinking in about twenty-five years. And thus, solve the population problem.

• • •

Dear Swami:

I've been working with a program called "Don't Mess With Texas" designed to keep people from disposing their trash alongside our beautiful Texas highways. In trying to come up with the appropriate penalty for littering, I decided to tap the wisdom of the centuries and ask you, Swami. What do you think?

Tanya Hyde,
San Marcos, Texas

Dear Tanya:

In order for justice to truly be done, the punishment must fit the crime. That's why I recommend that people who litter be crumpled into a little ball, tossed by the side of the road and left there to rot.

7

Everything I Eat Turns to Money and My Drawers are Full of Cash

Over the past several years, more and more people have become conscious of the relationship between mind and prosperity, the fiscal and the metafiscal. I don't know, perhaps it is because more ordinary middle-class citizens are having near-debt experiences, but folks are really beginning to examine their habits about money. So here I would like to offer my own 12-step program for Economic Recovery to heal our disfundsional economic system.

SWAMI BEYONDANANDA'S 12-STEP ECONOMIC RECOVERY PROGRAM

1. Admit that we have become powerless over debt, and our economic system has become unmanageable.

2. Admit that only a power greater than ourselves—greater even than Ross Perot—can help us overcome our unconscious debt-wish and restore fiscal fitness.

3. Admit that our denial of debt has put us where we are today. Cut up our credit cards and laugh in the face of debt.

4. Make a searching and fearless moral inventory of our economic system. Get down to the real needy-greedy, so to speak. Heed the need and lose the greed.

5. Become entirely ready for God—or the voting public, whichever

comes first—to remove all defective characters from positions of power.

6. Lower defenses and defense spending. Just say NO to the profits of doom.

7. Instead of trading insecurities, invest in our true wealth—our human and planetary resources.

8. Humbly ask God to tell Congress once and for all that pork ain't kosher.

9. Enact a tax sir-charge. Tax all of those excessutives who are making more annually than their corporation is. People are fed up with the fact that every time the economic belt gets tightened, the same old fat drips over the sides. And tax those illegal aliens as well. Anyone who can afford to come here in a spaceship can certainly afford to pay their share.

10. Make a list of all persons or institutions that we have harmed or ripped off in our ruthless pursuit of wealth. Tell the truth! In this game, our lie-ability is no asset. Anonymously pay them back. If these are people we really hate, all the better. Imagine them staying awake nights wondering who the hell is sending them money.

11. Continue to take personal inventory, and give away anything we are not using. Recycle. Let's cycle again instead of driving so much, and we'll trim our waist and our waste at the same time.

12. Remember that we are all responsible for our society's fiscal health. If our economic system goes belly up, default is our own.

• • •

Dear Swami:

I am obsessed with money, and I am determined to be wealthy, no matter what the cost. It's true that money can't buy happiness, but it can certainly rent it for a while. I've already tried your "Everything-I-eat-turns-to-money-and-my-drawers-are-full-of-cash" affirmation—and it works—but frankly with the kind of wealth that I desire, that's going to be far too taxing on the digestive system. I'm ready for the advanced course, Swami. Sock it to me.

Selma Soul,
Palm Springs, California

Dear Selma:

You sound like you mean business—you want to be even richer than your God-given intestines can provide. So I guess that calls for drastic measures, and I think I have just the thing. You need to consult the all-time expert in wealth-at-any-cost—Midas Welby-Rich. Welby-Rich made his first fortune as an informant during the McCarthy Era (a period described in more detail in his autobiography, Fink And Grow Rich), then made subsequent fortunes imparting his knowledge to anyone ruthless enough to listen. His later book, I Upped My Income—Up Yours!, describes the metaphysical aspects of acquiring wealth. "If you desire wealth above all else," Welby-Rich writes, "you must learn to conquer such weaknesses as ethics, integrity and compassion. You must live by the Golden Rule that has guided fortune-seekers since the first coin was pressed: 'Do unto others—then get a good lawyer.' If wealth is your only goal, you must mobilize all of your life energy—that which the Chinese call 'chi' (pronounced "chee")—toward that end."

*The use of chi or life force plays a significant role in Welby-Rich's best-known book, Chi Ting: The Principles of Unprincipled Wealth-Gathering. This book has greatly influenced the likes of Richard Nixon, Ivan Boesky, Jim Bakker, Leona Helmsley and other Chi Ting masters. Indeed, Chi Ting is widely practiced in the fields of finance, industry, politics, and even entertainment (yes, that TV show you enjoyed last night just may have been stolen from someone too naive to understand the **real** L.A. Law).*

A word of caution. Since Chi Ting involves deception, you must develop the ability to lie with impunity. Since few of us are born with this talent, you may have to take daily doses of Deniatol or hire an expensive attorney as lie-ability insurance. Like anything else, Chi Ting has its pros and cons. And judging by the above list, all it takes is one fraudian slip to turn even the most adept pro into a con.

• • •

Dear Swami:

A while back, you told us that we used to create our own reality, but now it's all made in Taiwan. I got to thinking about that, and I realized you're right. I mean, I live out here on the West Coast where there are a lot of Taiwanese immigrants, and you've never seen a harder working bunch. They seem driven to make something of themselves, even if they have to work two or three jobs to do it. I know you're not a sociologist, Swami, but I do value your insights. So, tell me. What in your opinion makes these people so industrious?

Phyllis Sofficle,
San Rafael, California

Dear Phyllis:

Most sociologists would tell you that it is due to many complex factors ranging from the influence of the ancient Chinese culture to economic pressures intensified by crowded living conditions. But as a Swami, I prefer the simpler approach. So I say it is because so many of them have that Taipei personality you hear so much about.

• • •

Dear Swami:

Many spiritual visionaries have long dreamed of a moneyless society. Do you believe we will achieve this ideal within the next decade?

Robin Banks,
Sedona, Arizona

Dear Robin:

Judging by the numbers of people I've seen lately living on the streets and on the unemployment lines, I'd say a lot of folks have already achieved the ideal.

• • •

Dear Swami:

A few years ago, I read one of those books like *Do What You Love, The Money Will Follow* or something like that. Let me tell you, I was inspired! That day, I quit my day job and decided to pursue my life's purpose—doing baseball card readings. Now I'm sadder and wiser. My business was a bust, and although I still believe my purpose is doing baseball card readings, customers are just not beating down my door. Creditors are, however. You know how sales clerks will say, "We take credit cards?" Well, mine have already been taken. What I want to know is, why hasn't the money followed? Or if it has, why hasn't it caught up? What can I tell you, Swami. I'm disillusioned.

Morty Feid,
Santa Monica, California

Dear Morty:

I understand perfectly what you're going through. It must be frustrating indeed to have finally found your place in the sun—and all you have to show for it is a terrible sunburn. I, too, went through what I call my Baroque period. I was so Baroque, I was Haydn from the landlord.

135

When I could Handel it no longer, I went to my guru, Harry Cohen Baba, who snapped me out of it. "You're disillusioned?" he said. "That means you must have been illusioned first." And then it hit me like a ton of affirmations. I had been so caught up in the vision, that I had neglected the details of my business. And each detail that is neglected grows bigger and bigger until eventually detail is wagging the dog. You see, we intuitive types tend to favor the right brain over the left. But you know what they say: When you make only the right brain right, the left brain gets left.

Fortunately, I've found a way to make a living—selling life purpose insurance to people like yourself. That's right, life purpose insurance. And the best life purpose insurance? Join my new organization, Ananda Nominational Church, and become your own religion. Not only are you tax exempt, but being a religion gives you permission to have sacraments, ceremonies and holidays—stuff that individuals are not particularly encouraged to do. You can go around asking for contributions to your building fund, and what are you building? A life of purpose, self-expression and service. I don't know about you, but to me a life fulfilled can be as beautiful as a cathedral—and its positive repercussions more powerful and longer-lasting.

• • •

Dear Swami:

I've got a number of friends who've recently gotten involved with network marketing programs, and I find myself avoiding them because (a) they're always trying to sell me something, and (b) they're trying to get me to sell that something to someone else. Sometimes I feel like I'm missing a great opportunity, but mostly I'm turned off by their single-minded determination to make a sale. Can you offer some perspective here?

Sol Etude,
Ventura, California

Dear Sol:

*It is true that becoming involved with a network marketing program can turn even the most evolved human being into a single-sell organism. But we must not overlook the possibility that this type of multi-level plan can also turn a financial 97-pound weakling with an anemic bank account into a superb fiscal specimen. It doesn't even matter what the product is. In fact, one very successful company is selling Spam multi-level. That's right. The company is called **Spamway,** and it's marketing Spam as the ultimate survival food because no matter what, it is guaranteed to be the last thing on your shelf.*

• • •

Dear Swami:

I understand you have learned the secret for making a small fortune in the stock market. Can you share it with us?

Bill Yanaire,
Hilton Head, South Carolina

Dear Bill:

Yes. Start with a large fortune.

• • •

Dear Swami:

The current Savings & Loan crisis—isn't it just one more indication that the banking system is crumbling? Some channels—and even a few radical economists—are predicting a complete banking collapse by 1995. Is there anything that can be done to restore confidence in our financial institutions?

Iona Kondo,
Vail, Colorado

Dear Iona:

*It is true, the S&Ls are in very serious trouble, so serious that they've even applied for welfare. And isn't it just like those bleeding-heart conservatives to fall for their sob stories and put them on the dole? Meanwhile, to bolster consumer confidence, the banks have come up with a simple and logical solution—enlist the expertise of confidence men. After all, developing new confidence requires new confidence schemes. Knowing full well the power of testimonials by famous personalities, one major bank is working on a TV commercial where a bearded figure in flowing robes strolls down Wall Street accompanied by celestial music. He turns and enters said bank as the words flash on the screen in Biblical script: **Jesus Saves.***

● ● ●

Dear Swami:

I've often heard inspirational speakers say that we should do what we love and the money will follow and all that, but I can never get any of them to say anything more specific about exactly how to do this. I love to write poetry, but I could never figure out how to turn this into a money-making activity. Swami, can you give me some practical advice?

Lotte Riewinner,
Madison, Wisconsin

Dear Lotte:

In a word, Amway. Amway is your key. Actually, not just Amway but any multi-level program that well-meaning friends are pestering you with. And the more you detest the idea of selling someone else's soap, the better it will work. Step one, invest a little money and sign up as a distributor for the organization. Step two, meditate on your sales kit daily. Imagine yourself taking valuable time away from your poetry to organize meetings, make endless phone calls, and look at every human being you meet as a potential customer. If that sounds like fun to you—and it may—you have found your calling. But if the endless calling doesn't call to you, I guarantee that after two weeks of considering the prospect of selling someone else's dream, you will mobilize all of your creativity and resources to pursue your own.

● ● ●

Dear Swami:

Tell me if you think this is fair. While I was in Canada a few months ago, I bought a brand-new Audi and paid the full Canadian taxes upon purchasing it. When I returned to the states and tried to register my car I found I had to pay over $1,000 in additional duty. I have appealed several times, and lost my last appeal yesterday. Any words of wisdom?

Yehudi Zervit,
Scarsdale, New York

Dear Yehudi:

Guess it's Audi duty time, eh?

● ● ●

Dear Swami:

Here's something I find puzzling. Why is it that when we already have a glut of unoccupied office space in most cities, developers insist on building more regardless of environmental impact? It seems like some kind of dysfunctional obsession, if you ask me. What's your take on this, Swami?

Norma Lee Mild,
Ann Arbor, Michigan

Dear Norma:

Yes, you're definitely on target. Quite often, people—particularly men—will end up building beyond what is needed. They think that if they keep building and building they will overcome their feeling of not being enough, and that what they construct will become their living monument. In psychological circles, this is known as an unresolved edifice complex. This worship of the man-made leaves millions of pilgrims stuck on the highway of life each morning as they religiously go to acquire practice. The result is what I call "greedlock"—the inability of society to move forward due to our faulty view that self-worth is a result of net worth.

Fortunately, there is a cure for greedlock and the unresolved edifice complex. And that is to divest. Take off that vest, and while you're at it, sever those power ties. Leave your mercenary life behind, and become an immercenary instead. Immerse yourself in an esteem bath, where you imagine your parents, teachers, and especially Ed McMahon telling you that you've been given a special gift just for entering—so you are already a winner!

• • •

Dear Swami:

As a retired person on a fixed income, I have to save money any way I can. That's why I've cut down to two meals a day. I eat breakfast at about 10:00 a.m. and have an "early bird special" dinner at the local all-you-can-eat buffet at about 5:00 before the prices go up. I'm wondering if there's any health risk in eating this way.

Moe Betta,
Ft. Lauderdale, Florida

Dear Moe:

I am sorry to have to report this, but a recent issue of the medical journal Lancet reports that for some unknown reason people who eat at early bird specials three or more times a week run a higher risk of getting worms.

• • •

Dear Swami:

I'm looking for the perfect investment, something which is guaranteed to go up. I remember reading that you had your own Wall Street advisor, a great prophet named Yuan Tibet. Could you ask him about the ideal investment?

Sasha Diehl,
Great Neck, New York

Dear Sasha:

Indeed, Yuan Tibet was a master of fiscal fitness, and being a Dowist, knew the stock market like the back of his nose. Unfortunately, he is unreachable and may no longer be on the physical plane. Last spring, it seems that there was a flurry of prophet-taking on Wall Street, and someone apparently took him. He has not been heard from since, but I know what he would say: "If you want to invest in the one thing guaranteed to go up, invest in taxes."

• • •

Dear Swami:

What advice can you give me on the money market?

Richard Denhue,
Arlington, Virginia

Dear Richard:

Well, I'm no expert but from personal experience I must say the money market doesn't look too good. Just a few days ago, I was surprised to see a guy actually selling money on the street. He was selling ten dollar bills for $8 and twenties for $15. I walked over and was surprised to find that these were real bills he was selling, not counterfeit. So I asked him how he could make anything selling money at those prices, and he replied, "Sure, I lose a little on each transaction—but I make up for it in volume."

• • •

Dear Swami:

I'm terribly embarrassed about this, but I'm one of those young people that you read about who's been forced to move back home because of financial problems. No matter how hard I try, I always seem to get fired from my jobs. I guess I can't tolerate pettiness, and it shows. With the economy as unstable as it is nowadays, I'd really like to change this pattern. What is your advice for getting hired and staying hired? And what encouragement can you offer a guy who's 33 and just moved back to his dad's house?

Mario Momma,
Akron, Ohio

Dear Mario:

You know, your problem may be purely astrological. You could be getting fired so much because you're a fire sign. So if you want to get hired once and for all, I suggest working on your hire consciousness. And remember, once you actually are hired, you may at times need desperate measures to save your job. I suggest—just for emergencies—you learn the heinie-lick maneuver. As far as moving back home, you're in good company. 33 is the exact age when Jesus went back to live with His Father.

8

Achieving an Altared State: Swami's Tips on Dear Hunting

Even though marriage is the leading cause of divorce (statistics show that 100% of divorced people were once married), people continue looking for that special someone to help them achieve an altared state. Yes, it is true. Dear hunting is the most popular sport in our society. Problem is, most people don't know what to do with their dear once they catch them. You can't very well mount them on the wall— unless you are very agile.

It is true that opposites attract. Men and women have been attracted to each other since the beginning of time. But attraction is just the first step. You see, people get attracted to each other and think they're going to live happily ever after. But just because there's a spark—or even a full-blown flame—doesn't mean there's a match.

Of course, when chemistry takes over, we forget all about our social studies. And then we may be very disappointed to find that our perfect match turned out to be just a flash in the pants. So the best advice I can offer is to relax, and remember that love is like baseball. You can hit a grand slam one day, and be shut out the next. So do not be discouraged, even if the boxscore reads, "No runs, no hits, no eros." Don't worry about scoring. Just try to make contact. Enjoy the game. Step up and take your licks. And whatever you do, don't just stand there looking. If you're going to strike out, at least go down swinging. And maybe if you're alert, you'll turn a single into a double.

• • •

Dear Swami:

I have a problem with self-esteem, especially when it comes to women. Whenever I come into contact with a woman I find attractive, I get very nervous. I can't imagine her ever being interested in me, so I withdraw. And there goes another missed opportunity. Can you relate to this, Swami? Any advice?

Ron Lykelle,
Ardmore, Pennsylvania

Dear Ron:

*Of course I can relate. I, too, in my younger days was shy with women. I remember being at a party once and mustering up my courage to talk to an attractive young lady. I asked her to tell me about herself, and she said she was involved with Special Ed. I was sunk. I thought to myself, if this guy Ed is so special, what does she want with me? That was before I learned the truth—that Special Ed was going steady with Amazing Grace. In fact, they used to double-date with Boneless Chuck and All-Beef Patty, which of course left Skinless Frank on his own. But I digress. Your problem is, you don't value your uniqueness. Think of how many billions of people have appeared on the planet since the starting gun went off. You are the only **you** who ever was and ever will be. That makes you rarer than the rarest diamond or pearl. And unless you start some weird sect in Idaho, only one lucky woman will ever be able to marry you. So stop hiding from her. See yourself as the prince you are and keep* *your eye out for your Cinderella. Next time you are at a party, don't be afraid to take out that slipper that fits only your intended. When you find a likely candidate, have her try it on. And if the shoe fits, rejoice for you have found your solemate.*

• • •

Dear Swami:

We are recently married, and each of us has been married before. We each remain on good terms with our respective exes, and expect to be friends with them for the rest of our lives. Some of our friends think there's something wrong with this. What do you think, Swami? Also, we want to make sure the excitement lasts in our new marriage. Any suggestions?

Joy & Matt Trimoni,
Huntington, New York

Dear Joy & Matt:

In answer to your first question, not only do I think staying friends with your ex is fine, but it is the wave of the future. I expect to see a lot more whole life ex-beaus in the coming years. As far as keeping the excitement in your marriage, I have read that enjoying all kinds of physical activity together can kindle that spark. So I suggest that every week you do laps together. As to whose lap gets done first, I'll leave that up to you.

• • •

Dear Swami:

I'm a young woman who was brought up in a strict family where we were told in no uncertain terms that the purpose of sex was procreation and procreation only. I have since switched religions, but I still believe in sexual purity and chastity. Problem is, every time I go to the beach to meditate I get distracted by all these gorgeous guys with skimpy briefs and terrific tans. How can I channel my energy into more spiritual pursuits?

Shirley I. Wood,
Long Beach, California

Dear Shirley:

What you face is a common dilemma. We are biological beings, and these natural urges demand release. And yet, society's mixed messages put us in a difficult situation. We're damned if we do, and dammed if we don't. And if we try to submerge the urge to merge long enough, the dam is bound to break. Then we get like poor Jimmy Swaggart, whose delusions of glandeur cost him his career. So enjoy the brief diversion. And don't be too concerned. Even the most spiritual young woman gets off on a tan gent from time to time.

• • •

Dear Swami:

I've been happily married for twenty-seven years, and I've always had a meal ready for my husband when he comes home from work—until recently. About two months ago, for no apparent reason, I lost all desire to cook. Just like that. This has been exasperating to my husband—and to me—but I can't bring myself to cook anymore. What's going on?

Juana Cruz,
San Luis Obispo, California

Dear Juana:

Not to worry. You're just going through menupause.

• • •

Dear Swami:

My husband spends all of his time at his office, and I just found out that he's been having an affair with his computer. Any advice?

> Nora Mance,
> Providence, Rhode Island

Dear Nora:

I know that your first instinct is probably to buy him a surge-sup-pressor. I suggest instead that you offer him more outlets. Perhaps if he got more bytes from you, he'd need less from his computer.

• • •

Dear Swami:

I've been reading your column and looking at your picture each month and I think you're really cute. I sure hope you're not one of those Swamis who practices celibacy. What I mean is, Swami, do you have sexual relations?

> Vanna T. Press,
> Salt Lake City, Utah

Dear Vanna:

Oh, I have some very sexual relations. My parents, for example. If they hadn't been sexual, I wouldn't be here today. As far as celibacy goes (and many people think it goes entirely too far), when I was younger I practiced it all the time. By the time I was 18, I had become so good at it that I didn't need to practice it anymore. Having mastered celibacy, I said, "Great. Now what else is there?" I figured with all the beautiful navels in the world to contemplate, why waste time on your own. Now while I am flattered by your attention and impressed with your taste, I must tell you that I am married. You see, I always fantasized making love to a married woman, so I decided to marry one and see what it was like. And that is all that I will say about my sex life. Last time I elaborated in print, I found my entire private life splashed on the pages of Bawdy Mind And Spirit magazine.

• • •

Dear Swami:

I've been searching for a tantric sexual union. Do you have any advice for me?

Vi Brader,
Allen Park, Michigan

Dear Vi:

Hey, I'm a union man, myself. I'd recommend joining Tantric Sexual Union Local 347, and that's just up the road in Inkster. But you know, I'm just not sure about all this spiritualization of sex. It used to be, you asked your partner if they enjoyed it. But with all these tantric people, the common question is, "Was it God for you?"

• • •

Dear Swami:

Perhaps you can help us with a very sticky problem. Two years ago, my husband and I bought a very beautiful summer home on Cape Cod. The problem is, last summer we were inundated by visiting relatives. Rich ones, poor ones, it didn't matter. They came in droves. Is there some way we can gently discourage unwanted visitors so we can have some peace and quiet?

Jennie Rossity,
Amherst, Massachusetts

Dear Jennie:

It just so happens I have a simple solution. When your rich relatives come to visit, borrow money from them. Then, loan that money to the poor ones. It's a sure bet you'll never see any of them again.

• • •

Dear Swami:

Several years ago, when I was younger and more headstrong, I married a man strictly because he was wealthy. Anything I wanted, he would buy for me. I thought that was enough, but apparently it wasn't. I'm bored out of my gourd, and despite the wealth, my life seems dull and stale. Unfortunately, there isn't much I can do but share my sad story. So, to anyone reading this column—remember, just because a guy can write a check, doesn't mean you're going to want to spend the rest of your life with him.

Ivanna Gohohm,
Palm Springs, California

Dear Ivanna:

You're absolutely right, and you're not alone in this problem. After all, you're not the first queen to get rooked on the chessboard of love. You were so determined to have a checkmate, that you ended up with a stale mate instead.

• • •

Dear Swami:

I've been going out with this guy for two years, and I just can't get him to make a commitment. Although he insists that he loves me, he also insists on having numerous other girlfriends. When I mention marriage, he laughs and says, "Real men don't get married." My therapist says he is suffering from a Don Juan complex. Can you explain?

Sharon Cheryl Ike,
Irving, Texas

Dear Sharon:

Yes. A Don Juan complex means he Don Juan to get married, he Don Juan to have responsibilities, and he Don Juan to grow up. Behind that macho exterior is an insecure little boy. The wolf act is just a disguise. He's a little lost sheep in wolves' clothing, following someone else's ideal of manhood. So I'd give him a taste of his own Don Juan stuff. Tell him you Don Juan to be with a sheep, you want to be with a man. And if he still Don Juan to own up to his insecurities, I'd tell Ram Beau to flock off.

• • •

Dear Swami:

I've noticed a lot of spiritual paths these days seem to be emphasizing the differences between men and women. I thought the new age was about androgeny, and that unisex is the wave of the future. Can you shed some light on this?

Marsha Lartz,
Santa Cruz, California

Dear Marsha:

Even though we are all One in Spirit, the physical Universe exists in dualities. And one of those dualities is female/male or yin/yang. Each of us has chosen to learn our lessons this time around by acting primarily through one of those dualities. In other words, some of us are in with the yin crowd, others are yang at heart.

A similar duality exists within each of our brains. There is the right—or intuitive—hemisphere, and the left—or logical—side. As a society, we are grossly out of balance. I know what they mean when they say ours is a left-brained civilization because judging from the mess we've made, we've obviously left our brains somewhere. Scientists say that the brain is a hologram, but in our society at present it's no more than a half-a-gram.

So the Goddess energy—that natural feminine impulse to love, nurture, and protect—is what is needed to restore balance. In order to go forward, we need more women expressing this energy in the political realm. Because when you have only men in government, do you know what you have? A stag-nation. And women acting as women—not as clones of men—have the power to make a great doe-nation and put us back in our right minds.

• • •

Dear Swami:

Can you comment on sex in the '90s?

Mary Ann Devorss,
Hollywood, Florida

Dear Mary Ann:

Sex at any age is terrific, but if you're in your 90s, just that fact alone should make it better. Remember, you're never too old to loin!

• • •

Dear Swami:

Didn't you find it ironic that the same week Magic Johnson announced he was HIV-positive, another former basketball player, Wilt "the Stilt" Chamberlain announced he had made love to 20,000 women over the course of his career? Perhaps Magic

151

Johnson's sobering news will take some of the glamor away from unbridled sexual expression. What do you think, Swami?

Germaine Mann,
Brooklyn, New York

Dear Germaine:

I agree with you about unbridled sex. While we cannot expect everyone to become practitioners of Transcendgenital Meditation, it is reasonable to expect sexually active young people to at least wear a—uh, bridle. And the irony you mention was not lost on this Swami. In fact, it inspired a poem which I hope will bring the point home:

WILT THE STILT

Wilt the Stilt, says his autobio

Was one amazing lover guy-o.

20,000 times he scored

Postgame behind bedroom doors.

20,000 passes, 20,000 dunks

(Who says Warriors have to live like monks?)

In those days of sexual revolution

Getting laid was no problem —It was the solution.

But scoring points by bedding maids

Is risky in this age of AIDS.

Is this evening's pet the one

Who'll be a loaded roulette gun?

One bad call could get you kilt

*Now **that's** enough to Wilt the Stilt.*

• • •

Dear Swami:

Please enlighten me as to the practice of sex while on the spiritual path? Is it proper?

Ron Chi,
Sausalito, California

Dear Ron:

Absolutely not! Having sex while on the path is very improper indeed, and must be discouraged. If you want to have sex, go into the bushes, go behind a sign, but not on the path, okay? It is very distracting to the rest of us.

• • •

Dear Swami:

Could you say somethimg about sexual addiction? What do you think is the cause, and is there a cure?

Lucinda Street,
Houston, Texas

Dear Lucinda:

*Good news for you. There is a treatment center in Houston that offers what they call "cold turkey" treatment. For three nights in a row, you go to bed with a frozen turkey. This usually does the trick. As for cause, I think people lust after sex because they didn't get enough non-sexual physical affection as children. This lack of affection made them feel unwanted, and as adults they are trying to meet this need for touch the only way they know how. In a recent survey, 80% of the respondents said the most satisfying sexual position is **cuddlingus.** Yes, it's true. What we really want out of sex is to have someone cuddling us! So maybe if every child experienced plenty of cuddling, they would wait to have to have sex—and we'd have fewer unwanted children.*

• • •

Dear Swami:

If I may be so blunt, Swami, my husband stinks. Literally. I mean, he's a good provider, a terrific companion, a decent lover but—well, let's say his food combining leaves something to be desired. We'll be in bed, all set for a romantic evening and all of a sudden this noxious gas will waft up from under the covers. I'll say, "Oooh. What did you have for lunch?" and he'll say, "I dunno. It escapes me right now." Funny, right? Except that I'm on the verge of leaving him for someone who's . . . a little less expressive. I want to do the right thing, Swami. Can you help me?

> Ada Lemma,
> Schaumberg, Illinois

Dear Ada:

Before you do anything rash, have a little compassion. Your husband is probably working something out on the gastral planes. You see, most of our emotional problems stem from having intestinal gas as babies and not being able to get rid of it. This condition is known as "Burp Trauma. Although some may think of this as a passing difficulty, it is something that will come up repeatedly unless released once and for all. Fortunately, there are techniques such as Gastral Projection and Reburping which teach you to let these painful experiences flow through you, so to speak, instead of holding them in. The great Native American shaman, Broken Wind, the developer of Reburping, maintains that the release of gas is the most natural thing in the world—in fact, it is our burp-right.

Now, just as each of us must choose our own path, so we must choose the path of release—what Reburpers call "the high road" and "the low road." While the high road is more socially acceptable in Western society, the low road is more fun to watch in a hot tub. So next time your husband sends a pungent cloud of cabbage perfume hurtling down that lower pathway, think of it as the release of a past trauma, a release that will clear his emotional body as well and allow him to more fully digest life's experiences. So I suggest you celebrate these emotional releases with your husband. For as Broken Wind has said, "To air is human, to forgive divine." And don't be tempted to stray just because you think the air is cleaner in someone else's bedroom. For in these days of glamor and image, perhaps the greatest challenge is to love the one you whiff.

• • •

Dear Swami:

This is a very sensitive issue, and I need your wisdom. My boss has been coming on to me for the past couple of months, and I've gently deflected his advances. But now I find myself in a real dilemma. We are going on an out-of-town business trip together, and he asked me to book adjoining rooms. I know this is a provable case of sexual harrassment, but I like my job (and my paycheck) very much, and the risk is simply too much for me. Any great suggestions?

Sue Dehrpantzoff,
Skokie, Illinois

Dear Sue:

I have often maintained that when you raise yourself to a higher level, harrassment becomes impossible. That is why I suggest you acquiesce to your boss's instructions and indeed book adjoining rooms. Book him in Room 1220, and book yourself for 1320.

• • •

Dear Swami:

Can you tell me where my ex-wife is living and what she is doing?

Stan Dalone,
Donora, Pennsylvania

Dear Stan:

I'm sorry, but I think you have me mixed up with some other swami. I don't do past-wife readings.

• • •

Dear Swami:

I thought I'd heard about every bizarre perversion there is, but now it comes out that in Italy the latest thing is for old men to make wooden puppets in the likeness of young boys. Do they have a name for this sicko behavior?

Bo Lingali,
Cleveland, Ohio

Dear Bo:

They sure do: geppetophilia.

• • •

Dear Swami:

I recently read an article which suggests that men also go through a "change of life" in middle age. This phase is reportedly characterized by worries about health, aging and decreasing vitality. Is there any truth to this notion of male menopause? Have they come up with a name for it yet? And is there anything

I can do to soften the blow of yet another affliction I have to look forward to?

Sid Down,
Athens, Ohio

Dear Sid:

It's about time somebody drew the logical conclusion that if women go through menopause, men must necessarily go through what can only be called "womenopause." And unfortunately, the number one symptom of womenopause is that—well, a man goes from being all paws to all pause. Fortunately, there is some good news. I recently saw a TV commercial for a new service which is designed to provide instant reassurance to middle-aged men in the throes of performance anxiety. It's called Club Med Alert. The commecial shows a hapless womenopause sufferer desperately punching up "B-4-S-E-X" on his cellular phone and shouting? "Help! I've just fallen for someone—and I can't get it up!"

• • •

Dear Swami:

You want to know my theory about why the world is so screwed up? It all has to do with orgasms. See, men's orgasms last what, about 30 seconds? Women, on the other hand, can have their orgasms go on indefinitely. Consequently, men are jealous and they've brought greed and destruction onto the world. Do you agree, Swami?

Lynne Schmob,
Seattle, Washington

Dear Lynne:

*Come on now. Even the most militant feminist can't blame **all** of the world's problems on men's shortcomings.*

157

9

More Hard-Pore Corn
and Homily Grits

People often ask me about my most unusual experience, and I find it very hard to answer because my whole life is unusual. In fact, if I ever had a usual experience, that would be unusual. But there are three experiences which come to mind. The first occurred several years ago when I mustered all of my courage (and available cash) and finally attended the Ascended Masters Golf Fantasy Camp. It's one thing to look up to your sports heroes as gods, but when your Gods are sports heroes, that's really something. Actually the first day was kind of a let-down. It was very, very boring because I got to play with three Zen masters. Everything took so long because first they had to hit the ball, then they had to not hit the ball. And so on.

The second day I was afraid they were going to put me with Moses. He is known for hitting the ball into the sand and then wandering 40 days till he hits it out. Fortunately, I missed playing with him. But to my shock, they make me part of an unforgettable foursome: me, Jesus, Mohammed and Buddha. And I got to tee off first. Was I terrified! I was so intimidated that I sliced my first shot into the rough. All of a sudden, I see this squirrel with my ball in his mouth running toward the creek. Next thing I know, an owl has swooped down and has lifted the squirrel by the scruff of his neck. As the owl flies over the green, he drops the squirrel, the squirrel drops the ball, and it gently rolls into the hole. All three of those Ascended Masters just kept looking up at the sky as if nothing unusual had happened, although I did catch Jesus giving me a little wink, that Sly Devil. Anyway, from that moment on I lost my nervousness and felt just like One of the Guys.

The second experience happened several years ago when I was invited to a formal affair in Washington, D.C. where they served soul food—chitlins, black eyed peas, corn bread and collard greens—covered with a spicy Siamese peanut sauce. I must have looked puzzled, because the waiter said, "What's the matter? Ain't you ever been to a Black Thai dinner before?"

The third incident that comes to mind happened just last summer in Dallas when I was invited to a cast reunion party for the Texas Chainsaw Massacre. A very unusual event, but I'll tell you—there was a terrific cross-section of people there.

Yes, the human mind works in mysterious ways. Particularly my mind. When I am reading or listening to a conversation, my mind meanders all over the landscape. I've often thought that I must be descended from that ancient people, the Meanderthals, for this very reason. For example, when I read about a father and his young son having what amounts to being a religious experience because their favorite hockey player took them out to dinner, all I could think about was the Father, the Son, and the Goalie Host. Or the time I saw a box marked "outgoing mail," and I wondered what happens to shy mail. Or my reaction when I first heard that the ashram of my guru, Harry Cohen Baba, was in Flushing, New York: "Hmm. Flushing New York. Not a bad idea."

Yes, I stay up many a night wondering. Sometimes I even wonder around in my sleep. When I hear about computerized weaponry, I wonder if someone will develop nerd gas. When I hear about a comedian who used to do impersonations but doesn't anymore, I wonder if he's a post-impressionist. Or if the Ascended Masters Golf Tournament is played on astral turf. Or if voyeurs in China are called Peking Toms.

So come a-wondering with me as we meander through the final chapter and graze on one last serving of hard-pore corn and homily grits.

• • •

Dear Swami:

Maybe I'm an old fuddy-duddy, but I've noticed standards are considerably lower nowadays than when I was a youngster. Is that true? I'd like an impartial opinion.

Ben Tehellenback,
Sun City, Arizona

Dear Ben:

You probably are an old fuddy-duddy. My dictionary defines fuddy-duddy as "anyone who uses the phrase 'fuddy-duddy' in conversation with normal human beings." But anyway, I, too, have suspected that standards have been lowered so I decided to investigate on your behalf. I checked with the National Bureau of Standards in Washington, and sure enough, a picture is now worth only 648 words, an ounce of prevention is worth a half a pound of cure, and a bird in the hand is worth just 1.6 in the bush. But there is some good news. Thanks to advances in beauty and personal grooming aids, if Helen of Troy were alive today, her face could launch some 1,750 ships.

• • •

Yo, Swami:

Could you say something good about rap music?

"Vanilla Ice Cream" Cohen,
Flushing, New York

Dear Vanilla:

Sure can. Rap music cannot be converted into Muzak.

• • •

Dear Swami:

All these nostalgic revivals—the '60s, the '70s—where will it all end? Will we still be listening to '60s music thirty years from now when we're all in retirement communities in the Sun Belt?

Horace Zontal,
Menlo Park, California

Dear Horace:

As a matter of fact, I just returned from a vacation in the future, and I had a chance to visit one of these retirement communes somewhere up in the Santa Cruz mountains. I think the year was 2021 or something like that, and sure enough some of those old, old groups were still touring. One show featured the Doddering Stones, the Huh? and the Grateful Near-Dead. It was just like Alzheimer's Day at Yankee Stadium. Bob Dylan made one of his surprise guest appearances, and amazingly his voice at 80 was just as smooth and resonant as it was at 25. Unfortunately, most of the audience had long since lost their hearing due to loud rock 'n' roll music, so all of the songs had to be translated in sign language. That was the cause of the evening's one tragic moment. An old fellow was furiously signing Dylan's "Subterranean Homesick Blues" and, well, he never made it past "Get sick, get well..."

• • •

Dear Swami:

I've been alarmed at the recent rise in serious crime in this country. Is there a bright side to this I'm not seeing?

Helda Genster-Will,
New York, New York

Dear Helda:

Yes, there is. Sure, serious crime is up, but funny crime is down. Did you know that over the past three years, incidents of bubble bath being put in shopping mall fountains has decreased 35%? And New York City, thanks to its highly successful "Turn In An Artist" program, has virtually eliminated the phenomenon of people painting mustaches on subway posters. And it's been over twenty years since some heartless pranksters caused a near-panic on the stock market floor by dropping dollar bills from a balcony. Why? Because cops always say, "Now don't try anything funny!" Obviously, this has worked. So if we want to eliminate serious crime, we just have to have cops say, "Okay, now don't try anything serious!" It's worth a try. It cannot possibly hurt, and it can't be less effective than what we're doing now.

• • •

Dear Swami:

I understand you visit Hawaii regularly, so maybe you can help me. Whatever happened to my favorite Hawaiian recording artist, Don Ho? Have you ever seen him, and if so, what is he up to?

Mei-Ling Liszt,
Palo Alto, California

Dear Mei-Ling:

Call it coincidence or call it serendipity, I just happened to run into Don Ho over the holidays, and he was promoting his new Christmas album, Ho Ho Ho Ho. He told me he'd just returned from New Orleans where he'd spent six weeks at a Howard Johnson's motor lodge recording a three-album set with Yoko Ono and cellist Yoyo Ma. The albums will be entitled Yoko Yoyo Mojo Hojo Ho, Mo' Yoko Yoyo Mojo Hojo Ho, and No Mo' Yoko Yoyo Hojo Mojo Ho. I said I could understand Yoko Ono, but wasn't Yoyo Ma a little too classical? He said, "Hey, there's always room for cello."

• • •

Dear Swami:

Are you psychic?

Faye Thealer,
Chapel Hill, North Carolina

Dear Faye:

You know, I knew you were going to ask that question.

• • •

Dear Swami:

I understand there are plans afoot for an all-nude cable TV channel. Have you heard anything about this? I am waiting with bated breath for your answer.

Al Fresco,
Boca Raton, Florida

Dear Al:

*Good luck. I tried baiting my breath once, but didn't catch anything but a sore throat. To answer your question, the idea for this **Cable Nudes Network** has been floating around for years. The main problem has been how to protect impressionable young children from being exposed to—well, from being exposed to. As a way of redressing the situation, the Network now has the technology to simultaneously broadcast an overlay of what looks like paper doll clothing to protect young eyes from visually explicit material. Parents simply use a code to activate the overlay when they leave their children at home. Then, as soon as the program comes on, a sign appears in the lower right-hand corner of the screen which says, "This program is clothes-captioned for the visually sensitive."*

• • •

Dear Swami:

Have you ever studied at one of the great Mystery Schools?

Hugh Dunnitt,
Monterey, California

Dear Hugh:

*Oh, yes. I spent a wonderful summer once at the **Agatha Christie Mystery School** and I learned a great deal. Even now, I am sometimes called upon to use my skill as a sleuth. In fact, I was recently called up to Battle Creek, Michigan, to help solve some particularly heinous crimes. I don't know if you heard about this—it was kept pretty hush-hush—but remember Snap, Crackle and Pop, those three cute little guys? Well, they were found face down in a shallow pool of skim milk. And shortly afterward, Cap'n Crunch fell or was pushed into a wheat shredder and came out as 47,800 bite-sized biscuits. And you remember the Trix rabbit? All they were able to recover of him was a rabbit's foot. The* authorities up there in Battle Creek were baffled, and I'm afraid I wasn't much help. "I don't have the slightest clue as to who might have done this," I told them, "but it sure looks like you have one of those cereal killers on your hands."

• • •

Dear Swami:

We all know that vegetarians eat vegetables, and as you yourself have pointed out, humanitarians eat humans. Now that you've written a book, Swami, aren't you a little concerned about authoritarians?

"Sly" Drool,
Cambridge, Massachusetts

Dear Sly:

There is always reason for concern because down through the ages, many creative people have been devoured by the authoritarians. In fact, that is why so many writers nowadays seek to protect themselves by having such bad taste. Personally, I am not that worried. I figure the Swami is too much for any authoritarian to swallow.

• • •

Dear Swami:

I have heard that, as a Humanitarian, you eat people. This sounds like it would get boring after awhile. What do you do for dietary variety?

Farrah Mount,
Ventura, California

Dear Farrah:

No, it doesn't get boring at all, especially since there's so much ethnic variety. Refried beings, Greek salad, and of course, my favorite dish—Spanish vegetarian omelet, which is quite expensive because Spanish vegetarians are extremely hard to find. And for that occasional Swede tooth, my guru Harry Cohen Baba introduced me to a seasonal favorite, Humantashen.

• • •

Dear Swami:

Whatever happened to that recent Latin dance craze, the Lambada? You don't hear much about it anymore.

Fonda Dieux,
Lafayette, Louisiana

Dear Fonda:

There is a good reason for that. The Surgeon General declared the dance a health hazard because some partners became so entwined that they needed to be surgically separated. As a matter of fact, I read about one New York surgeon who made a fortune doing nothing but lambadamies.

• • •

Dear Swami:

While at the airport recently, I picked up a very interesting book called *Amazing True Facts*. One of the stories that fascinated me was an account of the bombing of London during World War II. It seems that one block was bombed at least three times, and each time the only building left untouched was a Schick razor warehouse. Do you know anything about this story?

Roald Oates,
Front Royal, Virginia

Dear Roald:

I sure do. Apparently the legendary sturdiness of this building is at the root of the now-famous phrase, "built like a Brit Schickhouse."

• • •

Dear Swami:

I know you travel a lot on the astral planes, so I'm sure you can answer my question: Where is Elvis, and what is he up to?

Wanda Lust,
Fresno, California

Dear Wanda:

Elvis is doing great! He and Buddy Holly and Roy Orbison have hooked up and they've formed a new group called the Foreverly Brothers.

• • •

Dear Swami:

I've noticed in your live lectures and columns that you sometimes use old jokes. Is there a reason for this?

Faye Slift,
Ogden, Utah

Dear Faye:

Yes there is. I am known as the Environmental Swami, and when I notice a throwaway line tossed out, it is my instinct to pick it up. So I am not merely using old jokes. I am recycling.

• • •

Dear Swami:

Hey, you seem to be on top of these things. I hear Ronald Reagan is headed back to Hollywood to make one more picture? Any truth to this rumor?

Harry Storer,
Glenview, Illinois

Dear Harry:

I just thumbed through the prognostications issue of the National Enquirer, and since none of the 50 psychics polled predicted a screen return for Ronald Reagan, I feel fairly certain in saying that it will happen. Actually, I have it on good authority that the ex-President will be tapped to star in Reagan Hood, a semi-autobiographical tale about a mythical hero who works outside the law to redistribute wealth. In an '80s twist on the classical theme, this hero robs from the poor and gives to the rich.

• • •

Dear Swami:

What's the difference between yoga and yogurt?

Gustav Wind,
Fargo, North Dakota

Dear Gustav:

*Although both derive from ancient cultures, there the resemblance ends. Yoga comes from bhakti, yogurt from bhakteria. I think the mix-up comes from all those **I-Can't-Believe-It's-Yoga** studios that have sprung up across the country.*

• • •

Dear Swami:

I recently heard a rumor that there's a new movie being made about the Kennedy family. Have you heard anything about this?

Von Leiner,
Roslyn, New York

Dear Von:

I've checked with my usual Hollywood sources and they tell me that indeed a movie will be coming out next year about the Kennedys. Apparently, it's a real white-knuckler about a woman trapped at a party in the Kennedys' Palm Beach compound and it's called Dances With Wolves II.

• • •

Dear Swami:

I was recently watching a documentary about a Haitian shaman. I was fairly detached from the whole thing until I saw a segment where he stuck pins in dolls. At that point, I felt an eerie familiarity as if I myself had done this in the past. Any explanation?

Karma Kannick,
Sedona, Arizona

Dear Karma:

I'm not sure. Deja voodoo, perhaps?

• • •

Dear Swami:

My wife and I are having a disagreement. We're considering getting a dog, and I'm all for going down to the humane society to pick out a homeless mutt. She, on the other hand, is set on getting a purebred. In fact, she's ready to plunk down $800 for a Standard Poodle. I think that's ridiculous. What do you think?

Ty Yerdout,
Scottsdale, Arizona

Dear Ty:

I'm with you. For that money, she should at least get an automatic.

• • •

Dear Swami:

I think it's great that more folks are becoming healthy and sober, but sometimes I feel nostalgic for the bad ol' days of unsafe sex, drugs, booze, loud music and just plain being obnoxious. In my little town, for example, all the biker bars have given way to health clubs, the honky-tonks have become brain gyms, and the porn shops are selling recovery literature. Now don't get me wrong. I'm genuinely happy that there are fewer drunken drivers on the road, but sometimes I just want to "get wild" and there's nowhere to go. Does this strike a chord?

Lew Smorrals,
Greenville, South Carolina

Dear Lew:

Yes, it's true. As "civilization" expands, there is less and less room for wild life. And this is sad, in a way. While we may not want some drunken beast stomping around in our living rooms, that's no excuse for making it extinct. That's why I believe every community should have a Wild Life Preserve where folks can visit their animal selves and get wild every once in a while.

You see, so often "re-covery" means covering up those old impulses with a civilized veneer and convincing yourself that they have no place in your life. But do you know what happens? These impusles bubble under the surface until they burst out in really warped ways. Do you realize that every time the Bible Belt tightens a notch, another Satanic cult is born?

On a recent trip to the future, I was pleased to find that this Wild Life Preserve idea had been adopted by many communities—and it worked exceedingly well. By confining "inappriopriate behavior" to an appropriate place, communities were able to cut down on crime, violence, sexual assault, and drug and alcohol abuse. In fact, some communities even encouraged recovering alcoholics to get drunk once—and only once—a year, because they maintained that the only way to tame the wild horse of desire is by learning to ride it. While I was there, I attended the annual Rambo Gathering where men spent a week gruff, bellicose, unbathed and unshaven, having tug-o-wars and mudslinging contests, swilling beer and making disgusting bodily noises. I even stopped by a conference for enlightened call girls called the Ho' Life Expo, but that's another story. One thing about the Wild Life Preserves I visited was that no one gets hurt. Sex is safe, violence is managed, and drunks get put to bed in a clean room instead of a dirty doorway. Now this might upset some purists (I mean, <u>impurists</u>), but just as we protect nature in our nature preserves, it's only logical that we protect humans in our human nature preserves.

• • •

Dear Swami:

Is it true that inanimate objects have consciousness?

Stan Sturiesen,
Madison, Wisconsin

Dear Stan:

Yes, it is true. Inanimate objects do have consciousness and this is finally beginning to be recognized by our court system. In a recent Florida case, a woman's scarf was used to tie up a robbery victim. A psychic was able to plumb the consciousness of the scarf to help police find the perpetrator. In an ironic postscript to the story, the scarf was brought up on charges as well. Said the prosecutor, "Sure, the scarf cooperated with the authorities, but it's still an accessory."

• • •

Dear Swami:

Please give me an example of "perverse."

Moe Lester,
Mystic, Connecticut

Dear Moe:

Sure. "Perverse" is how poets get paid.

• • •

Dear Swami:

Do you ever get a chance to venture into the Spirit Realm and speak with people who have made their transition? I'm particularly interested in that great screen personality, Mae West. I used to really enjoy her, and I wonder how she's doing on "the other side."

William Issmee,
Beverly Hills, California

Dear William:

Funny you should mention Mae West, because I ran into her at a recent Ascended Masters Golf Tournament. It turns out her consciousness has been completely changed since her transition, and she's become very "new age." In fact, she's got a new opening line: "Is that a crystal in your pocket, or are you just glad to see me?"

• • •

Dear Swami:

A lot of my friends are real excited about "Virtual Reality." In case you're not familiar with the concept, you can now have all kinds of experiences and adventures without ever leaving the comfort of your computer screen. What do you think, Swami?

Tina Peale,
San Francisco, California

Dear Tina:

I think it makes sense, particularly in a society that has figured out how to have safe sex, decaffeinated coffee, non-alcoholic beer, and low fat ice cream. We have intestinal bypasses, heart bypasses, and brain bypasses (i.e., daytime TV). So of course, the next logical step is the Reality Bypass. Indeed, in my own informal polls most of the folks I ask about Virtual Reality say, "Well, it sure beats the heck out of real reality!" I've also discovered that a lot of those twenty-something folks who used to frequent singles' bars now engage exclusively in "virtual sex" with their computers. But rather than resolving sexual issues, this practice has created new questions: Should I indulge in sex with multiple partners and risk losing all my programs to some deadly computer virus? Should I commit to just one virtual partner? Will my computer respect me in the morning? Some practitioners have even suffered bouts of what my friend St. Silicon calls "p.c.-ness envy"—wondering whether some other guy has more RAM than they do. Add this to the inevitability of someone coming home unexpectedly and finding their best friend logging onto to their virtual partner—and you can see that we haven't really progressed much at all. But the bottom line for me is that I cannot enthusiastically look forward to a day when *Get A Life!* becomes an advertising slogan for some computer program.

• • •

Dear Swami:

Here's a question that has always puzzled me. Why do men have nipples?

Phil Landerer,
Miami, Florida

Dear Phil:

*This question was raised at a recent scientific symposium and the consensus was that men's nipples are simply decoys to attract **other** nipples.*

• • •

Dear Swami:

I've got to know. Are these real questions from real people, or do you make them up yourself?

Bertha Von Aeschin,
Fredericksburg, Texas

Dear Bertha:

We make up all of our own questions—including this one.

Other Books from Aslan Publishing

Gentle Roads to Survival
Making Self-Healing Choices in Difficult Circumstances
by Andre Auw, Ph.D.

Psychologist Andre Auw, a close associate of the great 20th-century psychologists Carl Rogers and Virginia Satir, characterizes people who learn to prevail over life's challenges as survivors. Using dozens of case histories, poems, and allegories, Auw identifies the lessons all survivors know: characteristics that distinguish people who give up hope from those who find the inspiration and encouragement to carry on.

$9.95

The Heart of the Healer
edited by Dawson Church & Dr. Alan Sherr

In this brilliant book, chiropractors, doctors, cancer surgeons, nurses, psychologists—even priests and mystics—share their deepest insights into the healing process. These 19 authorities—**Bernie Siegel, Larry Dossey, Norman Cousins and others**—talk intimately and personally about the strengths and weaknesses of the healer and how these affect every person they touch.

$14.95

If You Want to Be Rich & Happy, Don't Go To School?
Ensuring Lifetime Security for Yourself and Your Children by Robert Kiyosaki

In powerful, no–nonsense language, Kiyosaki shows the root fallacies on which everything from our grading systems to our school hours are based, and demonstrates that we must make simple but radical changes in our approach if we are ever to prepare our children for the gifts of financial security and balanced, happy lives.

$22.95 hardcover

Intuition Workout
A Practical Guide to Discovering and Developing Your Inner Knowing
by Nancy Rosanoff

This is a new and revised edition of the classic text on intuition. Lively and extremely practical, it is a training manual for developing your intuition into a reliable tool that can be called upon at any time—in crisis situations, for everyday problems, and in tricky business, financial, and romantic situations. The author has been taking the mystery out of intuition in her trainings for executives, housewives, artists and others for over ten years.

$10.95

Magic at Our Hand
Releasing Our Lives into Order & Beauty
by Nancy Exeter

Amid the familiar, there are moments when a different dimension is sensed, and we may marvel at the way a resolution has come, or catch our breath at a beauty we cannot describe.

Nancy Exeter, in a book which is as much a work of art as a work of prose, here expertly reveals the essence of the universal feminine in everyday life. With a gentle, clear voice, she calls you to an awareness of the exquisite beauty to be found in every moment if you will only be aware.

$11.95

Other Books from Aslan Publishing

Marsha Sinetar in Conversation with Michael Toms

Marsha Sinetar is the best-selling author of *Do What You Love, The Money Will Follow* and *Living Happily Ever After*. In her work as an organizational psychologist, she has studied many people who have become successful doing what they love. In this new book, she speaks to those who are attempting to live their deepest calling in the midst of a seductive world. She emphasizes that **choosing a lifestyle which blends inner truth with work, family and the demands of twentieth century life** is more than possible—it's essential!

$8.95

Fritjof Capra in Conversation with Michael Toms

Fritjof Capra is the author of the international best-sellers *The Tao of Physics* and *The Turning Point*. In this book he takes us with him on his remarkable personal journey into the nether realms of quantum physics, where the traditional worlds of science and spirit twist and merge to the point where the distinctions become blurred. As he relates his wisdom-packed interactions with leading contemporary thinkers and visionaries, we discover some of the new ways of thinking and being that are moving us towards the millennium, as "the rising culture" brings sweeping social changes to the global human society

$8.95

Personal Power Cards
by Barbara Gress

A simple, easy-to-use set of flash cards for emotional wellness. Includes 55 cards, a carrying pouch, and an 80 page booklet. The cards help retrain your feelings to be positive and healthy. Their combination of colors, shapes, and words allow positive thoughts to penetrate deep into your subconscious, "programming" your emotions for health.

$18.95

Winds Across the Sky
A Love Story
by Chris Foster

Every so often a novel comes along that is simple, magical, utterly unique and compelling. *Winds Across the Sky* is that kind of rare, exceptional work. In beautiful, simple language, it tells the interweaving stories of an ancient redwood, a humpback whale, a burned-out Vietnam veteran, and a French-Canadian movie star. Its magical climax is a triumphant affirmation of the interconnectedness of all life forms.

$12.95 hardcover

Your Body Believes Every Word You Say
The Language of the Body/Mind Connection
by Barbara Hoberman Levine

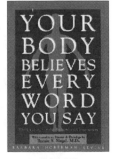

Our best-selling health title describes the link between language and disease. Levine's fifteen-year battle with a huge brain tumor led her to trace common words and phrases like "that breaks my heart" and "it's a pain in the butt" back to the underlying beliefs on which they are based and the symptoms they cause. With over 25,000 copies in print, this book is on its way to becoming one of the classics of modern healing literature.

$11.95

Order Form

Date_____

Name _____

Address _____

City _____ State_____ Zip_____ _____

Phone _____

Please send a catalog to my friend:

Name _____

Address _____

Item	Qty.	Price	Amount
Gentle Roads to Survival		$9.95	
The Heart of the Healer		$14.95	
If You Want to Be Rich & Happy Don't Go to School?		$22.95	
Intuition Workout		$10.95	
Magic at Our Hand		$11.95	
Marsha Sinetar in Conversation with Michael Toms		$8.95	
Fritjof Capra in Conversation with Michael Toms		$8.95	
Personal Power Cards		$18.95	
Winds Across the Sky		$12.95	
Your Body Believes Every Word You Say		$11.95	
		Subtotal	
	Calif. res. add 7.25%	Sales Tax	
		Shipping	
		Grand Total	

Add for shipping:
Book Rate: $2.50 for first item, $1.00 for ea. add. item.
First Class/UPS: $4.00 for first item, $1.50 ea. add. item.
Canada/Mexico: One-and-a-half times shipping rates.
Overseas: Double shipping rates.

Check type of payment:

☐ Check or money order enclosed

☐ Visa ☐ MasterCard

Send order to:
**Aslan Publishing
PO Box 108
Lower Lake, CA 95457**

Acct. # _____

or call to order:
(800) 275-2606

Exp. Date _____

Signature _____

WYS